Casting with
LEFTY KREH

Lefty Kreh
photographs by Jay Nichols

STACKPOLE
BOOKS

Published by
STACKPOLE BOOKS
5067 Ritter Road
Mechanicsburg, PA 17055
www.stackpolebooks.com

Printed in China

10 9 8 7 6 5 4 3 2 1

First edition

Library of Congress Cataloging-in-Publication Data

Kreh, Lefty.
Casting with Lefty Kreh / by Lefty Kreh ; photographs by Jay Nichols. — 1st ed.
    p. cm.
Includes index.
ISBN-13: 978-0-8117-0369-7 (hardcover)
ISBN-10: 0-8117-0369-X (hardcover)
1. Fly casting. I. Nichols, Jay. II. Title.

SH454.2.K697 2007
799.12'4—dc22

                                         2007042082

To my daughter Victoria and son Larry.
No dad and mother could have two more loving children.

Contents

Acknowledgments

So many people helped make this book possible. No one did more than Jay Nichols, who helped me with the photography, did the original editing, and, being a fine fly caster and fisherman, was able to suggest important things I might have forgotten or overlooked.

I believe that one of the most important portions of the book is the chapter written by my fly-fishing friend Dr. George Yu concerning how improper casting strokes can cause tennis elbow, torn rotator cuffs, and other physical problems. What makes it even more understandable are the superb drawings by Gene Hansen and Doug Judy.

I am indebted to Judith Schnell, who encouraged me to do the book, and to Amy Lerner, who made sense of the more than 1,000 color photos and text.

Introduction

Good casting is easy. I don't mean that it comes easily—it doesn't. It requires a lot of hard work, practice, and time on the water fishing. What I mean is that good casters expend very little effort making most casts. My main goal in this book is to show you how to cast—whether you are young or old, male or female—without exerting any more effort than is necessary. Watching a young, strong caster huff and puff to send a fly line 100 feet doesn't impress me. What I look for, and take great pleasure in watching, is someone who casts well with as little energy as possible. Cathy Beck, for example, who weighs about 135 pounds and is perhaps 5'4" tall, can often throw the line farther than men twice her size, and with less effort.

The traditional method of fly casting teaches the angler to use mainly the arm and the wrist to make all casts. Most of the casts are made in a vertical plane, where the rod tip moves back and forth between the often-quoted 10 o'clock and 2 o'clock positions. This works fine when casting light lines, rods, and flies at relatively short distances. But when throwing longer casts, especially with heavier rods, lines, and often weighted or air-resistant flies, this method is not only inefficient, it can cause serious physical problems, such as painful tennis elbow or torn rotator cuffs. Since it requires strength, this method also prohibits older anglers and women who don't have powerful wrists and arms from expanding their horizons into saltwater or bass fishing, which requires heavier tackle and longer casts.

If you watch several of the best baseball hitters, each has a different stance and holds the bat differently when up at the plate. But despite these individual styles, all baseball hitters are captive to certain principles of hitting. To hit a home run, they swing the bat through a long stroke; to bunt, they use a short stroke. It is the same with casting. We, too, are captive to basic principles, and if we don't adhere to them, our casting and fishing success suffers. I realized in the late 1970s that people are built differently and fishing situations vary, so I stopped teaching the popular method of casting and began to teach basic principles. These are not my principles, they are physics. Once you understand these fundamental fly-casting laws of physics, you can improve your cast, adjust casting

The best casters expend very little energy making most casts. Above, Lefty Kreh casts tight loops with a bamboo rod and a large fly.

There is no one way or style of casting simply because anglers are physically different, fishing situations vary, and fly fishers use many kinds of tackle and flies. Above, Dave Whitlock casting on the White River in Arkansas.

strokes to your physical makeup, or adapt them to a specific fishing situation. There is no one way or style of casting simply because anglers are physically different, fishing situations vary, and many kinds of tackle and flies are used. You shouldn't cast a dry fly the way you would a weighted Clouser Minnow or a sink-tip line. The casting problems on a small trout stream, a big steelhead river, and a windy saltwater flat are so different that a single method or style of fly casting simply won't work in a variety of situations. Fly fishermen should learn to cast in many ways. Learning to cast one way means you can only fish one way, and you will miss opportunities. I think what is holding back fly fishing more than anything else is the lack of better fly casters. If people could cast better, they would buy more tackle, they would go fishing more often, and they would enjoy the sport more because they would catch more fish.

Many of these casts are applicable in a wide variety of situations, so I encourage you to read through the entire book, even if at first a particular chapter doesn't seem to pertain to you. For instance, even if you are only concerned with casting 50 feet, the chapter on distance casting can help you cast 50 feet more efficiently. If you fish for trout, the chapter on strip-

> *All the directions in this book are for right-handers. Points that I consider to be really important are in boxes like this one.*

ping baskets, which many anglers only consider a saltwater tool, might inspire you to try them on trout streams. Some casts that I have organized under "casts for weighted flies"—the low-side-up cast or curve cast—can also be used with dry flies.

In this book I hope to not only help you improve your fly casting, but also to better understand fly-casting mechanics and how to adapt them to various fishing conditions. I also want to emphasize the importance of learning how to prevent—or cast with—torn rotator cuffs and tennis elbow problems. Conventional methods of fly casting really strain these body parts, and as I've gotten older, I've come to realize how important it is to use all of your body to help make the cast. Not only is it easier, but it also prevents harm. I met Dr. George Yu, who is a fly caster and a renowned surgeon, while trying to find a solution to my own rotator cuff problems, which weren't caused by fly casting, but sure limited my ability to cast at times.

When I first met Dr. Yu, he asked me, "How do you sleep?"

I replied, "Not worth a damn."

He said, "No, I mean *how* do you sleep?"

Above: Flip Pallot casts incredibly narrow loops to probe under mangroves for snook. Captain Steve Huff poles the boat along a backcountry shoreline in Florida's 10,000 Island.

Below: Bob Clouser works the edge of a Susquehanna River grass bed for smallmouth bass. Casting large bass bugs and streamers all day can be hard work if you do not modify your casting stroke.

Cathy Beck's perfect casting form allows her to cast farther and more efficiently than casters twice her size and strength. Good casters who also fish a lot realize that efficiency is more important than strength.

I told him, "I'm telling you, George, not very well."

"Let me rephrase that," Yu said, smiling, but also a little impatient. "*Before* 'not very well' how did you sleep?"

Finally, what he was getting at dawned on me. "Well, I slept with my hand underneath my head."

"Well, Lefty, that's probably what caused your rotator cuff to tear."

He proceeded to explain to me that when you sleep like that, you stress the rotator cuff over time and partially tear it. At the time, I could not lift my arm 4 or 5 inches without bad pain. Dr. Yu gave me some injections, and by the end of the week, I realized that, for the first time in a long time, I could reach into the cupboard without pain. I had three more treatments, spaced two weeks apart, and I was like new. I had no idea that I could do such damage while sleeping. This is worth looking into if you have similar problems. Dr. Yu is a very busy man, so I am grateful that he took the time to contribute a much needed chapter on the medical point of view of fly casting and rotator cuff problems, which have been a persistent problem in our sport.

The more I learn about certain physical limitations to fly casting, the more interested I have become in trying to solve problems that plague many participants in our sport, or problems that prevent people from participating in our sport. Fly fishing grew in the late sixties in Florida when inventive and resourceful anglers faced conditions for which no previous cast had been developed, so they invented one to catch the fish. When George Harvey needed to sink his nymphs faster and without drag, he invented the tuck cast. Today, our casting repertoire continues to expand as more and more anglers are learning about Spey casting. (Simon Gawesworth and others have produced fine books on the subject, so I have not gone into it here, but I urge you to explore these techniques and continue to grow as casters. Just about every Spey cast with a two-handed rod is equally useful with a one-handed rod.) Fly fishing and fly casting are in constant evolution, and every day we add to what we know.

CHAPTER 1

A Lifetime of Learning

JOE BROOKS

In the late 1940s, I lived in central Maryland and I really didn't know anyone who fly-fished, except for one man, Sam Gardner, who dapped for brook trout in the tiny mountain streams in the Blue Ridge Mountains. In 1947, Joe Brooks called me and said that he'd like to write a column about bass fishing on the Potomac. Brooks, who at that time was not nationally known, wrote a weekly outdoor column for a small newspaper called the *County Paper* in Towson, Maryland. By that time, I had gotten a reputation with some of the better bass fishermen in the area as someone who knew how to catch fish with light plug-casting gear. (Even though spinning reels had been around in different parts of the world for some time, they were just coming into the United States.)

We went to the Potomac River just below Harpers Ferry, and I carried my 13-foot aluminum canoe down to the bank. I went up to get the rest of the gear, and when I came back down, I watched Joe assemble what I would later learn was an Orvis Battenkill fly rod and a GAF line, which was equivalent to a 9-weight line today. Because Harper's Ferry was at a cut in the mountains, there was always a little bit of a breeze, and that day was no exception.

"Joe, if you don't have a plug rod with you, I have an extra one," I offered. I was fishing with 6-pound braided silk line thin as sewing thread, and Joe had that fly rod with line that looked as big as rope.

"What do you mean?" he said.

"Well, it's kind of windy," I said. Bear in mind I had never seen a fly caster before.

He said, "Would you mind if I used this fly rod?"

"Not at all," I said, with doubts that it would work very well for him.

As we floated downriver, Joe caught almost as many fish on his fly rod as I did, which really impressed me. I had fished the river for years before and after the war, and I knew it well. After breaking for lunch, Joe walked upstream of a slanted rock ledge that ran parallel to the river, where he began casting to dozens of little rings on the water's surface. At first, I didn't think the rising fish were bass—I thought they were minnows. The fish rose, and he dropped the fly right into the ring, and caught a nice smallmouth. I couldn't believe how accurate and effective he was. He did this about eight times, and I thought: "I need to learn more about this." I later learned that every late September and October the Potomac gets a migration of flying ants that attempt to cross the river from Virginia into Mary-

Joe Brooks fishing for bonefish at Key West, Florida.

1

Joe Brooks holding an 18-pound mutton snapper caught on a fly in Key West.

land. Millions of them fall into the water, causing the bass and other fish to go on a feeding spree.

The next day, I drove to Baltimore to see Joe, and he took me to Tochterman's Sporting Goods where he helped me pick out a green, 9-weight South Bend fly rod for a GAF line (which today I wouldn't want to have to cast) and a Pflueger Medalist reel that I still have. He took me over to a park, and he gave me a casting lesson. While he didn't put a book under my arm to keep my elbow close to my body, which was the way a lot of old timers learned to cast, he taught me the typical 9 o'clock to 1 o'clock stroke. His elbow rose only a little bit and dropped a little bit. Watching how effective Joe was at catching fish with a fly, and his subsequent casting lessons, opened my eyes to a new dimension of fishing.

SMALLMOUTH

After my first lesson with Joe, I began experimenting with a fly rod on my own, for my favorite species—smallmouth bass. My stepfather had a boat on the Potomac at Lander, which is about 20 miles south of Harpers Ferry. I'd often fish for smallmouth there. I could get the popping bug or streamer out there alright, but only to distances of about 45 feet. I had already learned from fishing lures that the longer you could swim the fly through the water, or the more targets you could reach, the more bass you were going to catch. I quickly realized that moving your rod from 9 o'clock to 1 o'clock wasn't the best way to cast these larger flies long distances, and I gradually started to cast more toward the side and extend my arm farther. I didn't know any of the mechanics, but I knew that if I took that rod behind me, I could make longer casts with less effort. This revolutionized my casting and helped me catch more fish.

I began to show people the fish I caught (in those days we kept all of our fish) and what I caught them with. People did not believe that I caught them on a fly rod with popping bugs and streamers. I'd be on the river and overhear people say, "What is that guy doing, what is that big thing that he's throwing out there?" It was such a curiosity to people that people commented on it at the time. People then thought that you only fly-fished for trout, they didn't realize that you could also fly-fish for bass. Gradually, word got out, and I had

Casting for smallmouth bass during a blizzard hatch on the Potomac River.

maybe twenty guys in the local Frederick, Maryland, area where I lived who began to seriously fly-fish with me, and they formed a cadre of people that helped spread fly fishing, especially for bass.

It wasn't long after these first forays into casting that I learned to double haul from little diagrams in the *Wise Fishermen's Encyclopedia*, which was edited by A. J. McLane. I went to Cullers Lake in Frederick, laid the book on the ground, and learned to double haul from the diagrams in that book. Once I combined the double haul with extending the rod, things really started coming together. Had I just been a trout fisherman, I probably never would have modified the stroke that I first learned from Joe Brooks to help me cast farther and swim the fly through longer distances on bass rivers like the Potomac and Susquehanna. One of the reasons I began to develop the methods I did was that there really weren't a lot of anglers fly-fishing for bass to influence me. I had no one to give me advice, which, in retrospect, turned out to be just fine.

OUTDOOR WRITING AND PHOTOGRAPHY

Brooks was a mentor and gave me a range of good advice in my outdoor writing career—everything from never use a big word when a small one will do, to the importance of getting out and learning about other fisheries. Before Brooks, American fly fishers thought an exotic fishing trip was driving into Canada. In the 1950s, Brooks was fishing for everything from tiger fish in Africa to brown trout in Argentina and New Zealand, and he made us all realize that there was a world of fly fishing outside of America. He did his share of promoting within the United States as well—jump-starting the bonefishing and tarpon in the Florida Keys and publicizing Montana trout fishing, so much so that the governor of Montana bestowed on him the title of "Mr. Montana." Brooks was the guy who got us thinking outside of our local waters.

Back in the 1950s I was not making much money working at the biological warfare center in Fort Detrick, but I was earning some extra income writing outdoor columns for the *Frederick News Post*. At the time, there were probably only ten outdoor columns in the United States, and only four magazines on hunting and fishing. There wasn't much information available for folks. Bergman and one or two others had trout fly-fishing books out, but there probably weren't two dozen modern books available on fly fishing. When I started the outdoor columns, they took off, and I began writing for more and more papers. Most magazines commissioned illustrations or artwork, so when I began submitting photographs with my writing, it gave me a jump-start with the outdoor magazines *Sports Afield*, *Outdoor Life*, and *Field and Stream*.

In the mid-1950s, I realized that a lot of outdoor writers lacked knowledge about areas outside of their local stomping grounds. The outdoor writer from Georgia may know Georgia very well, but he doesn't know about stripers in New Eng-

land, Atlantic salmon in Iceland, or steelhead in Idaho. I realized that I needed to travel. I began giving seminars and clinics because they would pay my travel fees, and I would always stay over two or three days and fish with the local experts, learning their methods. Fishing with so many good anglers made me realize that casting requirements varied. If you were casting tiny little 3-weights for trout, you'd only need a short, little stroke; if you were trying to throw a bass bug way back in the brush in Alabama, or you were trying to throw to a steelhead in the Clearwater River, you might have to make a totally different cast. I realized that casting had to be different depending on the situation. Through these clinics, I was able to fish around much of the United States, and many parts of the world, and in 5 to 7 years I was able to get a handle on many of the different fishing methods in fresh and salt water. I discovered many casts and fishing techniques that I would find use for around the world, and since I was still traveling quite a bit and fishing different parts of the country, I

The first use of a white painted rod for casting photography in the 1973 book *Fly Casting with Lefty Kreh*.

continued to tuck away techniques learned on other waters. And I was also able to gradually learn something about how to teach and how best to explain casting to people.

At first, when I went to outdoor shows (not to clinics specifically for fly casting), my goal was to show as many people possible what they could do with a fly rod. During the fifties, Ted Williams and Jack Sharkey were doing outdoor shows with a lot of trick casting, such as writing names with a fly line, or they would both get up there together and create a "hatch." I used to knock a cigarette out of a woman's mouth at 60 feet, cast eight fly rods at one time, cast two rods and switch them in midair, and other stuff like that. It was meant to entertain, and also to convince people that I knew something about fly casting. One day I realized that this wasn't helping anyone. It was entertaining for sure, but not very instructional. I realized that if I were to show them how to improve their own casting—get rid of a tailing loop for instance, or throw a slack line cast, roll cast better, and so on—they would benefit more. After 5 or so years of these tricks, I started to focus more on showing people something that they could apply to their own fishing. In the end, I also think that teaching, instead of entertaining solely, was more impressive. If I could teach someone to make a side roll cast at 40 feet under a brush pile, that was much more impressive (and challenging) than knocking a cigarette out of a woman's mouth, which was just a casting parlor trick. I'd look out into the crowd, watch people taking notes, and feel proud that they were listening to what I was teaching them. They wouldn't have been doing that if they were just there to be entertained.

In the early sixties, Bill Ray, the managing editor at *Outdoor Life*, wanted me to write an article on my method of casting—he told me that it was revolutionary and that he hadn't seen anyone taking his arm back like that before ("Fly Casting with Ease," published by *Outdoor Life* in 1965). I agreed, but only if Ned Smith was to illustrate it, because we didn't have high-speed cameras back in those days. Ned Smith, the famous wildlife artist, who used to live in Halifax, Pennsylvania, was a very good friend, and his best friend, Jack Miller, and my best friend, Irv Swope, would fish the Susquehanna. Back then, there was still a lot of coal mine acid, so you didn't catch many fish, but what fish you did catch were usually big. So I went up there with Irv Swope, and we had dinner with Jack Miller and Ned Smith. After dinner, I made the proposal to Ned, and he was interested in doing it. As I started to tell them all the things that I wanted to photograph, they started smiling, and as I continued, began laughing at me: "You're not doing any of those things. You know how to cast, that's for sure. But you don't know what you are doing."

Of course, I tried to defend myself. To figure things out, we went out on the river with multiple cameras. Irv, Jack, and Ned all held a camera in a line, and one, two, three, they would all fire in succession, trying to get a motor-drive effect. When I printed the pictures out, I realized that I wasn't doing

Irv Swope casting to smallmouth bass on Maryland's Monocacy River.

a lot of the things I was saying I did. It was a major break-through for me, because I started monitoring and analyzing every cast that I made to understand exactly what I was doing. I still do that today.

Fly Casting with Lefty Kreh (Lippincott, 1974) was my first book, and it was the first instance I know of using rods painted white for casting photography. My friend Irv Swope shot the photos. Since then, I have been fortunate enough to publish many books on casting and fishing techniques, learning something from every one of them.

FLORIDA

When I went to Florida in 1964 to interview for the job as the director of the MET, the largest fishing tournament in the world, I had stories in *Outdoor Life*, *Sports Afield*, and *Field and Stream* all in the same month. I was publishing articles and newspaper stories with some regularity on both fishing and hunting. Vic Dunaway wrote a big article in the *Miami Herald* about this fishing "expert" from up north who was coming down to run the MET, in which he listed many of my accomplishments. They had some real hotshot fishermen down there, and that article really raised their hackles. They thought anyone north of the Broward County line couldn't fish, and I'm sure they thought, who the heck is this guy? They immediately invited ("challenged" is a better word) me over to do a casting demonstration—to see what I didn't know.

I knew that I had to make a good impression. Brooks had told me that the key to making good at the tournament I was to run in Florida was to get the light tackle (fly and spin) clubs down there to accept me. So I accepted the "challenge," and I went. After their regular meeting, we walked outside into the back alley, and under the streetlights, I laid the rod and line out onto the macadam. Without the rod, I picked up the line with my hands. As they all stood there with their arms crossed, I made a haul back and a haul forward, and cast the line. As the line unrolled forward, every one of them stepped out one step to see how far the line had gone—and I knew I had them.

From that point on, they knew they had more to learn. Most of those guys could catch fish on fly, but they didn't understand fly casting. After this first demonstration, word went out, and every evening, club members would show up at my house after dinner and cast in the cul-de-sac outside of my house. Chico Fernández, Flip Pallot, Paul Bruun, John Emory, Norm Duncan, and many others would come and cast and also share much with me about their innovative fishing techniques and methods.

As manager of the MET, I was fortunate to fish with many of the early pioneer and innovative fishing guides who were legends—Cecile Keith and his dad, Jack Brothers, Jimmy Albright, George Hommell, and many others. Every one of them shared their knowledge with me because I never told anyone in South Florida where they took me fishing. I learned so much from these great guides and friends.

Lefty and a barracuda.

Joe Brooks did much to publicize the fishing in Florida, and saltwater fly fishing began to really take off. In the late 1950s, Joe Brooks told Allen Corson, the outdoor editor at the *Miami Herald*, that he was going to go out and catch a bone-fish on a fly. Bonefish had been caught on a fly before, but no one had announced that they were going to go out and deliberately catch one. Joe went out and caught his bonefish, and he started writing about fishing for that species with a fly. This started a new wave of fishing in Florida with flats boats, and anglers began to catch bonefish and tarpon from boats. Fly fishing was evolving rapidly. New species and new water bred new techniques and methods of casting. Every time fly fishers met new fishing conditions, they had to tailor and develop casts for those conditions.

In 1965, another surge in saltwater fly fishing occurred when the Saltwater Fly Rodders of America was formed. As more people started fly fishing in the salt, the demand increased for good casting rods. Rods designed for trout were no longer good enough. Manufacturers started to produce the equipment necessary to cast to and catch saltwater fish like bonefish and tarpon. Flats boats were developed, as were

motors that would get you on plane and drive through grass, which formerly shut the engine down. Fly rods were developed with faster actions (they were fiberglass still, but vastly improved) that helped us cast tighter loops and fish more efficiently in the salt, better reels were made with good drags, and fly lines were vastly improved (the process changed, allowing manufacturers to design different tapers less expensively) and started to come in different colors, brighter ones that that we could see better. We could now travel great distances over the shallows that once were impassable, and then use tackle that did the job. It was a special time. Anglers competing with one another in the light tackle clubs came up with innovation after innovation such as teasing fish, new drag designs for spinning reels, new rod designs, and many new techniques. More things were developed and improved in light tackle in Florida between 1960 and 1970 than in any other period in this sport. And I was lucky enough to be right in the middle of it.

Above: Flip Pallot guiding a woman fishing Florida Bay flats for redfish.

Left: Stu Apte fishes the Florida Keys in the mid-1960s. He's wearing the doctor's mask to prevent sunburn.

CHANGING METHODS OF CASTING

In the late 1980s, I was L. L. Bean's photo and fly-fishing consultant, and once every fall I would teach a two-day outdoor photography seminar. It was a pretty intensive two days—a whirlwind of slides and photography pointers. A little old lady in tennis shoes—Mrs. Moberly—was a repeat student who took copious notes. I was talking about something, and all of a sudden she raised her hand.

"Yes, Mrs. Moberly?" I said.

Pointing her finger at me, she said, "Lefty, that is not what you said last year." All of the students grinned.

I thought for a second. I could hear some of the students chuckling. "Mrs. Moberly, if your instructor didn't learn anything between last year and this year, there's something wrong with your instructor," I replied.

She sat there, and stroked her chin, and you could see her mulling this over. Finally, like she was a judge commuting my sentence, she pointed her finger at me again and said, "I'm going to accept that." Everyone in the class broke out laughing.

In "How to Cast a Fly with Ease" (*Outdoor Life*, 1965), Irv Swope photographed me making a cast that looks very different than what I teach now. Here's a synopsis of how I describe the casting motion in this method:

> Lower the rod tip toward the water and remove all slack. Raise the forearm just above eye level (keeping a firm wrist) removing all line from the water. Make a short backward hammer stroke that lets the rod tip travel only about 18 inches. After this hammer stroke, let the rod drift back so that it is parallel with the ground. When the line straightens behind you, bring the rod butt forward until it is in front of you, with the entire rod still parallel with the ground. With a swift, but smooth motion, bring the rod tip over, and in the same area where you made the power stroke on the backcast, make a hammerlike blow. Stop the rod tip quickly, so that it points above the target.

At the time, I was trying to teach readers to travel far back with the rod (drifting back parallel to the ground or water), and I wanted to convey the idea that you accelerate to an abrupt stop, hence the hammer metaphor. Before that time, I knew of no one who was extending the rod this way, and I thought that it was worth writing about because of how effortlessly I could make long casts. Over the years, I have discovered that drifting in this manner, and even using the hammer analogy, is not the best way for me to teach fly casting. I found that with the hammer analogy, people still tended to use more wrist, so I have since used analogies like throwing a dart or flinging a potato off a stick, and, for tight loops, visualizing throwing the line at the rod tip. The pictures show that the rod is parallel with the water on the backcast and to get it there,

Teaching how to tighten loops, Cockeysville, Maryland, 2007.

my wrist is bent, and my elbow is elevated almost as high as my shoulder. Before that time, very few anglers ever took the rod back that far, and this technique showed them that by doing so, they could cast farther with ease.

Today, some tournament casters and young guns going for distance still cast in a similar manner, and while it may be an effective technique for distance, I think it is an inefficient one. This technique takes thousands of casts to learn to stop in the vertical position and then drift the rod without deforming the loop. It is critical that the loop unroll far enough away from the rod before you begin to drift back, or you are pulling some of the energy of the cast toward the ground behind you. Even once you master this technique, however, it is more difficult to make a lot of fishing casts from that backcast position, such as the stack cast, skip cast, and many others. Plus, even though you are moving the rod through a wide arc in the casting stroke by bringing the rod parallel to the water or ground, you can move it through an even greater distance by coming back sidearm and extending your arm behind you.

Most of the modern distance casters who use these drifting techniques have evolved from tournament casting, and many still belong to casting clubs, which I think are great and good for the sport, but a different animal than actual fly fishing. My analogy between tournament or club casting and fly-fishing casting is the same as trap shooting and upland game hunting: In both of them you use a gun, but in trap shooting, you tell them when to release the trap, and it travels at a set rate and pretty much at a set distance. When you are in the field hunting quail or grouse, you don't know how fast they're going to fly or at what angle they are going to go away from you. Though I don't think there are lots of similarities between tournament casting and fishing casting, tournament casters have given anglers many great techniques, such as the double haul, and innovations like shooting heads.

I have found over the years that instead of trying to explain the concept of drift to my students, which may or may not work for them, I tell them to go as far back with the rod as they want to go, and just stop. They don't have to learn through thousands of casts how to stop, drift, and begin their forward cast. They just need to learn how to stop, and by stopping with their arm back for a long cast, they become more efficient.

When I wrote that article over 40 years ago, I was younger and stronger, but I had not yet learned how to cast with maximum efficiency and with less wear and tear on my arm and shoulder. I think one of the most important benefits of teaching is that it forces the teacher to learn more. Many of the things that I have learned about fly casting came from seeking the answers to my students' questions. By the seventies, I had changed my method of teaching casting to base it on solid principles, which students could apply to their individual fishing needs.

Part I

FOUNDATIONS

CHAPTER 2

Principles, Casting Aids, and Other Key Concepts

Every casting stroke has two parts: a relatively long acceleration back or forward and a speed-up-and-stop. All good casting strokes begin slowly and continually accelerate, and the longer the cast, the longer the acceleration and line speed. The greater stroke length bends the rod more deeply, storing additional energy in the rod, and gives you the option to make the cast almost immediately or anytime while your rod hand is moving forward. When you don't move the rod back far, timing the forward cast becomes more critical.

At the end of a good casting stroke (on either the backcast or forward cast), the rod tip rapidly accelerates and stops suddenly. You can deliver more powerful casts by combining a longer stroke to increase line acceleration and the additional energy stored in the deeply bent rod. Speed, not power, deter-

mines the efficiency of the cast. We will talk more about this critical point later. In this book, I refer to this final casting motion, sometimes called the power stroke, as a speed-up-and-stop.

The basic casting stroke is the same with fly, surf, plug, or spinning rods. The only difference is that you unroll the line toward the target when you are casting a fly. And "casting," in my opinion, is misleading. We cast lures and bait on spinning or plug tackle, but a fly line is *unrolled* to the target. If you are not shooting line, any line that is straight from the rod tip out is not moving, similar to tracks on a tank. The tracks on the bottom of the tank are stationary and the tracks on the front end are moving and pulling the tank along. The closer that the forward end of the line (nail knot) is to the stationary part of

When "casting" a fly, you are actually unrolling the fly line to the target. When people think of casting the line, they tend to put too much effort into the forward stroke and overpower the cast. Terms such as "power stroke" sometimes make people think they need to apply a lot of power to the cast. But this power, if not applied smoothly, can produce energy-stealing shock waves in the line. Thinking of unrolling the line tends to deliver a smoother cast. If you unroll the line in a wide side or vertical loop, much of the cast's energy is dissipated around a curve and the line encounters more air resistance, diminishing the efficiency of the cast.

the line, the tighter the loop. When fly fishers think of *casting* the line, they tend to overpower the rod hand, which creates shock waves and other problems. Think of *unrolling* the line, and your presentations become smoother.

The most efficient cast has high speed and a small loop that unrolls directly away from and then directly toward the target. Large vertical or side loops distribute the cast's energy around a curve and not to the target and are more air-resistant than small ones. Another way to say this is that the larger the loop you unroll, either to the side or vertically, the more atmosphere the line goes through. People don't think that air makes anything, but when it blows toward you, it's wind.

> *When fly fishers think of casting the line, they tend to overpower the rod hand, which creates shock waves and other problems. Think of unrolling the line, and your presentations become smoother.*

THE PRINCIPLES

All sports have principles that you must follow, but individual athletes accomplish their tasks in different ways. In fly casting (and other types of casting as well), we must abide by four basic principles (fundamental truths about casting), even though we have different needs and purposes. As individuals, we are physically different. Even among people who weigh the same, one person may have longer arms or be more pow-

erfully built. Fly fishermen seek a huge variety of species under vastly different conditions. One angler fishes a narrow mountain brook and uses a tiny 2-weight rod and a delicate line to present a small Parachute Adams to a wary brook trout in shallow, air-clear water. Standing at the stern of a rocking offshore cruiser might be a fly fisherman throwing at a sailfish or marlin. Another angler may offer a huge Dahlberg Diver to a husky jungle peacock bass, while a steelhead fisherman will be casting a long two-handed rod and pattern with bead-chain eyes a great distance across a big British Columbia river. Waist deep in the surf, another fly fisherman bucks the stiff breeze with weighted line and a heavy fly to striped bass.

Because of these differences, no one method of fly casting is correct. Recognizing this in the late 1970s, I gave up teaching fly casting using conventional muscular movements and instead began to teach principles students could adapt for their physical makeups. Later they would be able to use these same principles to solve fishing problems and challenges as they arose. The principles that I teach are not mine. They are physics. The advantage of the four principles is that you can adapt

You cannot begin a cast until you move the end of the fly line. The same principle applies to plug and spin casting. The four casting principles apply to all casting with fly, plug, or spinning tackle. The only difference is that with plug and spinning tackle on the speed-up-and-stop of the rod tip, a weight pulls the line toward the target area. With a fly line, it unrolls to the target.

Once you understand the four principles of fly casting, you can use them in many fishing situations. For example, when you tie on a new fly, a small amount of line and leader lie on the water in front of you. Principle one says that you can make a cast once you move the end of the fly line. Drop the newly tied fly to the water, lower the rod, and make a series of wide back-and-forth motions parallel to the water. Don't make short strokes—they may tangle the leader. As you wave the rod tip back and forth, watch the end of the fly line. When it begins moving, you can make a backcast and deliver the fly.

them to your physical build (no two people can really cast exactly alike), you can adapt them to your fishing situation, and you can analyze and correct your own cast. These principles are not based on particular motions, because not everyone can make the same motions. You should never cast the way your instructor casts. You should cast the way that suits your physical makeup.

Principle 1

You must get the end of the fly line moving before you can make a back or forward cast.

To get the end of the fly line moving, you need to remove all the slack from the line. If your line is not completely straight in front of you, some of your lifting motion is used to pull the line straight before the end starts moving. This is wasted effort, and if you cast before you remove all the slack from the line and get the line end moving (drifting in the current doesn't count), you lose some of the benefits of accelerating the rod, and shock waves may develop in the line.

Place a garden hose on the lawn and put a single wave in it to resemble a potential sag in your backcast. Pick up one end of the garden hose and begin walking while looking at the other end of the hose. You won't move the far end of the hose until the large curve has been removed. Now position the hose so that one end runs straight for a ways and at the other end forms a large U-shape with the hose so that it resembles a backcast with a huge loop. Pick up the straight end and begin walking. The tip of the other end of the hose does not move until the larger curve has been removed. Both of these experiments demonstrate the importance of backcasts and forward casts with no sag and tight loops.

While it is not a casting rule, it is good fishing technique to lift all of the line from the surface before making a backcast. Ripping a fly line from the water can alert or frighten nearby fish and waste casting energy as the line is pulled free of surface tension. You should not make a backcast with any line lying on and below the surface. Quietly lift a floating line from the surface before the backcast, and roll cast sinking lines to the surface before making a backcast. This same principle applies to plug and spin casting—you cannot make a cast with a plug if there is slack in the line and the plug is stationary.

Picking Up Line Incorrectly

Lower the rod tip to the surface of the water.

As I lift the rod quickly while the fly line is on the water, surface tension grips the floating fly line.

Ripping the line loose from surface tension creates a huge disturbance. Even a short length of fly line from a quiet surface can alarm nearby fish.

I still make a backcast, but the damage has been done.

Picking Up Line Correctly

To pick up line quietly, lower the rod tip to the surface and remove all slack in the line.

Slowly raise the rod to draw the line closer.

Concentrate on the end of the fly line as you raise the rod. If you raise the rod too slowly, the line will sag and the end will never come free of the surface. If you raise the rod too fast, you rip the line from the water, disturbing fish. Only practice will teach you how quickly to raise the rod.

When the line end leaves the surface but the leader is still in the water, make a backcast while the rod tip is rising to ensure there is no sag in the line.

A good backcast with little disturbance on the water.

Principle 2

Once the line is moving, the only way to load the rod is to move the casting hand at an ever-increasing speed and then bring it to a quick stop.

A good casting stroke begins slowly, but smoothly and decisively, gradually accelerating to an abrupt stop. The sudden stop at the end of the cast is often called a power stroke, but applying "power" can spoil the cast. Instead, at the end of the acceleration, briefly move the rod hand even faster and then stop it abruptly. The stop is critical in delivering the full energy of the cast toward the target. Any immediate follow-through of the rod after the stop opens the loop and reduces line speed.

Instead of "power stroke" or similar terms, I use the term "speed-up-and-stop" to describe the period in which you accelerate the rod to a dead stop in the casting stroke. The speed-up-and-stop is one continuous motion, so I like to hyphenate the term when writing about it to try and convey that it is all one motion. The faster you accelerate the rod hand in the first portion of the casting stroke and the faster the hand speeds up and stops, the more energy the rod stores and the faster the line travels. As you speed up and stop, the rod tip does not travel in a straight path; it moves in a slight arc. The distance your rod tip descends from the beginning to the end of the speed-up-and-stop determines the size of the loop. If you make a long speed-up-and-stop where the tip drops 3 feet from the start to the end of the stroke, you get a 3-foot loop. If your stroke is short and the tip only drops 4 inches, your loop will only be 4 inches.

The stiffer the rod, the more potential energy it can store, and the farther back the rod bends, the more energy stored in the rod for the moment you stop it. As you move the rod forward, if you accelerate a short distance (even with a spinning plug or lure), you only bend the top of the rod and therefore only store energy in the tip, which is the weakest part of the rod. As you accelerate forward, the fly line gains speed. An easy way to demonstrate this is to have somebody hold the end of the fly line in his thumb and first finger while you bend the tip of the rod; he can hold the line easily. Then if you walk forward a few more feet and bend the rod more deeply, you can pull the line right out of his hands. This applies to both the forward cast and the backcast.

Principle 3

The line will go in the direction the rod tip speeds up and stops—more specifically, it goes in the direction that the rod straightens when the rod hand stops.

Once the rod straightens on the stop, you cannot change the direction of the cast—you could throw the rod away and the line will still go in the direction of the stop. It is somewhat like shooting a gun. Once you pull the trigger and the bullet leaves the barrel, you could throw the gun away and the bullet will still travel to the target. Or once you throw a ball toward a target, the path of direction cannot be changed. Understanding this important principle will help you monitor casting mistakes and adjust your stroke for different fishing situations. Some claim the line follows the path of the rod, which is true, but that rule is not applicable to fly fishing. Anything that you do to the rod after you stop doesn't affect the direction of the loop. If you lower the rod, the line is lowered, but the fly still goes toward the target.

As the loaded rod sweeps forward, it bends under the strain of pulling on the line. During the speed-up-and-stop, the rod unbends or straightens, determining the direction of the cast. If the rod stops abruptly and while the tip is rising, all of the cast's energy travels toward the target and does not

Because the rod was well extended behind me and the rod hand traveled straight toward the target with rapid acceleration, the rod is deeply loaded.

The line goes in the direction the rod tip speeds up and stops. For an elevated backcast, to prevent your line hitting the water behind you, you must speed up and stop with the rod tip going up.

sag. If you follow through even slightly after the speed-up-and-stop, the tip dips downward, you'll see sag in the line close to the rod, and some of the energy is directed downward and away from the target. Remember Principle 1? If there is a sag in the backcast, you can't begin the forward cast until you remove the sag and much of the forward motion with the rod is wasted on removing that sag. Without sag, the moment the rod moves toward the target the forward cast begins.

With most forward casts, you should speed up and stop with the rod tip slightly rising. If a tip stops going slightly downward, a larger loop occurs and sometimes causes the fly and line to crash to the surface.

When attempting to make accurate casts with weighted flies such as bead-head nymphs, weighted Woolly Buggers, even bonefish patterns, many tend to tilt the rod slightly so the weighted fly won't hit them on the forward cast. Right-handed casters tilt the rod to the right. But on the stop the tip will flex slightly to the left, and since the line goes in the direction the tip stops, the weighted fly will curve to the left as it falls to the water. It is amazing how many people using weighted flies don't notice this. To get the most accurate forward cast, the rod tip should travel vertically and stop in the direction of the target.

When helping someone cast, I like to talk about what the hand is doing rather than the rod tip, because the rod tip is 9 feet away and a lot of people have a hard time visualizing it. Making slight movements with your rod hand can move the rod tip quite a bit. If you grip the rod and bend your wrist back and forth, the rod butt only moves a few inches, but the tip is moving through a wide arc—perhaps 4 to 6 feet.

> *Slight motions with your rod hand are amplified at the rod tip. To cast tight loops, keep a firm wrist.*

Principle 4

The longer the distance the rod travels on the back and forward casting strokes, the less effort is required to make the cast.

A short back or forward rod stroke only bends the tip of the rod. As the rod moves through a longer stroke, the fly line continues to build line speed and increase the bend of the rod. What this means is that a caster with a shorter stroke must exert more effort to obtain the same line speed and load in the rod.

A fly rod is a flexible lever, and the farther back you bring it, the more it helps you make a cast. When making a short cast, you do not need to move the rod back far. When you have to cast farther, throw heavy or wind-resistant flies, defeat the wind, or make a number of special casts (even when trout-fishing small streams), bring the rod farther back and forward.

The longer stroke also has the benefit of giving you more time to pull out any slack in the line. You can't make a forward cast until you move the line end. If there is a shock wave in the line, or the wind pushes against the line creating slack, that slack must be removed before a forward cast begins. The longer the rod travels forward, the more slack can be removed. If the rod stops near vertical, less slack can be removed and the cast become more difficult.

Not only does bringing the rod back farther help load the rod, being able to take the rod well behind you on the backcast allows you to make many different casts. Fly casters should perfect their vertical, angled, and side casts to accommodate various fishing situations.

Because the rod has not extended back, the forward motion of the rod has little chance to remove any imperfections in the line so a forward cast can be made.

With the rod extended well behind, the angler can pull out any imperfections, and once the line is moving, the cast can be made sooner or later. Starting with the rod well behind reduces the critical timing between a back and forward cast.

AIDS TO CASTING

Whether you cast an ultra-light trout rod, a beefy tarpon rod, or a 14-foot two-handed rod, stance, thumb position, and keeping the elbow on the shelf will aid your cast.

Stance

Footwork is as important in fly casting as it is in other sports. Proper stance allows the body to better participate. When you are casting, your body should be able to move fluidly. When a right-handed person throws a stone a short distance, he unconsciously places his right foot slightly to the rear. But if he wants to throw the stone farther, he positions the right foot farther to the rear. These motions are natural. If you are right-handed, you should position your right foot behind you and your left foot slightly forward when you cast. Left-handers should do the reverse. This allows the body to swivel and the arm to easily move back and forth on longer casts, reducing strain on your rotator cuffs. If you cast a small dry fly 30 feet with a light line, you do not need to position your foot too far behind you. But when throwing a heavy fly, weighted line, or casting a long distance, the farther you place your foot behind you, the easier the cast.

> *If you are right-handed, position your right foot well behind you and your left foot slightly forward. Left-handers should do the reverse. This allows the body to swivel and the arm to easily move back and forth. On longer casts, it reduces the strain on your rotator cuffs.*

Casting Stances

When making a very short cast, you do not need to place your foot behind you, especially if you have sure footing. When fishing in fast-moving water or on a boat deck, you may want to spread your legs apart for balance, but it is not essential to aid your cast.

When casting a medium distance, spread your feet a little wider so that your body weight is evenly distributed between the two feet. As you make the backcast, shift your weight to your rear foot. On the forward cast, swivel your body and shift your weight back to the front leg, while accelerating the forearm to a stop and making a short haul on the line.

Place your rear foot farther back for a longer cast. This permits the rod arm to reach farther back and also allows the body to swivel more and aid in casting. The thumb is behind the rod handle away from the target, and the elbow is on the shelf. The rod is tilted almost 90 degrees to the side. Hauling aids the cast.

Bring the rod back to the side, drawing the line nearer. When the line end leaves the water, make the backcast. As you bring the rod back, swivel your body and shift your weight to your rear foot. Your forearm helps in accelerating the rod, but your body should be doing most of the work. This eliminates any strain on the rotator cuffs, and since you are not flexing your wrist, you decrease the likelihood of developing tennis elbow. The line hand is hauling on the line during the acceleration.

Stop hauling at the same time as you speed up and stop. Keep your wrist straight throughout the cast, and your elbow on the shelf. For longer casts, the body swivels until the chest is almost at 90 degrees from the target and the rod arm almost fully extended after the speed-up-and-stop.

As you turn your body and sweep the rod forward, shift your weight from the back to the front foot. There is virtually no movement or strain on the rotator cuffs. The line hand is hauling on the line during the rod's acceleration. Throughout this motion, the elbow should stay on the shelf, though with extra long back and forward casts, you may raise it slightly at the end.

Move your hauling hand up to just in front of the rod butt before making the forward cast. Swiveling the body, hauling, and moving the forearm accelerate the rod forward.

Stop hauling at the same time that you stop the rod.

Thumb Opposite the Target

Before you begin the backcast, position your thumb behind the rod handle, opposite the target. (Some special casts require twisting the wrist, such as vertical curve casts, but they are exceptions.) The most efficient cast is when the line unrolls directly away from and then unrolls directly toward the target. A large line loop (vertical or horizontal) dissipates energy away from the target. Most of the time, twisting the wrist will cause the line to unroll outward, wasting energy. Unless carefully controlled, flexing the wrist during the casting stroke enlarges the loop—wasting energy. The less the wrist is flexed when fishing heavier tackle or making longer casts, the less likely the angler will develop tennis elbow.

> *Before you begin the backcast, position your thumb behind the rod handle, opposite the target. The most efficient cast is when the line unrolls directly away from (180 degrees) and then directly toward the target.*

If you change the angle of your forearm, keep your thumb behind the rod handle from the target. For example, if you follow a side backcast with a vertical forward cast, lay your forearm and rod to the side, making sure your thumb is behind the rod handle away from the target. At the end of the side backcast, bring your forearm and the rod to the vertical position so the cast begins with your thumb behind the handle away from the target. All of the energy of the backcast will be directly away from the target. The higher the backcast is elevated, especially on longer casts, the more energy is wasted when changing the direction of the forward cast, which should be slightly rising most of the time. The forward cast should concentrate as much energy as possible toward the target.

Many fly fishermen throwing long distances develop twists in the line. Rotating the wrist outward on the backcast is often the cause. The line traveling back to the side is brought around for a vertical cast, producing a small twist in the line.

Thumb Opposite the Target

Your thumb should be behind the rod handle away from the target as each back or forward cast starts. This is the correct thumb position for a vertical cast.

To make an angled cast, do not twist your wrist. Instead, move your forearm to keep the thumb behind the rod handle from the target.

To make a side cast, lower your forearm and still keep the thumb behind the rod handle from the target. If you make a side backcast and a vertical forward cast, do not twist the wrist. Lay the forearm over with the thumb correct and make a side cast. Move the forearm up to make a vertical forward cast.

Incorrect: Bent Wrist

Bending the wrist even slightly can move the rod tip a great distance, causing wide loops. In the following sequence, I am making a short overhead cast, but I am bending my wrist. Note how my thumb isn't opposite the target.

This short overhead cast gets off to a good start.

I bring the rod forward with my wrist cocked and rod hand high. During the speed-up-and-stop, my wrist bends forward to straighten and my rod hand begins dropping, forcing the rod tip to throw the line around a large curve, and a big loop develops.

The rod comes up to the vertical position.

Note how far the rod sweeps downward, causing a wide loop.

My wrist bends, my hand is high, and my elbow left the shelf as I make the backcast. Because I bent my wrist and swept the rod back and down on the backcast, the speed-up-and-stop was long.

Incorrect: Bent Wrist

Here is a wide-angle sequence of the same problem to show how bending the wrist in this manner creates wide loops.

I begin the cast with the rod tip low to the water and start to raise the rod.

As I lift line from the water, I start to raise my rod hand and begin the speed-up-and-stop with my rod hand high and wrist beginning to flex back. A large loop typically develops when casting in this manner.

My wrist continues to flex. By the time the speed-up-and-stop ends, the rod tip has traveled around a wide arc, creating a large loop.

My rod hand is high as the forward cast begins.

As I sweep the rod forward, I begin to straighten my bent wrist. The rod hand has dropped considerably during the forward cast, creating a large loop.

The cast ends.

Straight Wrist

Here is a close-up sequence of keeping a straight wrist. The less you bend your wrist during the casting stroke, the tighter your loops.

Begin lifting line from the water. Keep a straight wrist and your rod hand low as it moves back.

As the rod hand travels straight ahead, begin a brief speed-up-and-stop.

Begin the speed-up-and-stop with the wrist barely flexed and the rod hand low.

The barely flexed wrist straightens and the rod tip stops straight ahead, not traveling down, which creates a smaller loop.

The rod tip travels a short distance during the speed-up-and-stop, and the rod hand has been kept low.

Duck the rod tip to prevent a tailing loop by pointing your thumb parallel to the water.

Straight Wrist

Here is a wide-angle sequence to show how a straight wrist helps make nice, tight loops.

Begin the cast with the rod tip low.

As you lift the line from the water, keep your hand and elbow low as the rod continues to lift the line.

Speed up and stop to make the backcast, keeping the forearm and hand low with little or no flexing of your wrist. The speed-up-and-stop is very short.

Because the speed-up-and-stop was short, the rod tip stopped directly away from the target, and I flexed my wrist little or not at all, the line is straight and the loop tight.

Begin the forward cast just before the line unrolls.

The low rod hand carries the rod straight forward toward the target. The speed-up-and-stop is brief with only the slightest flexing of the wrist so the tip stops parallel to the water.

This forms a tight loop.

Because my rod hand moved almost parallel to the surface during the back and forward cast and I flexed my wrist little or not at all, almost all the energy was directed away from and back to the target in the form of a small loop.

Twisting Wrist

If you hold the rod so that your thumb is vertical during the backcast, your body stops the rod hand when your forearm reaches vertical. To compensate for this limited range of motion, some people twist their wrists outward so that they can take the rod farther back. But this causes the line hand to unroll the line outward and energy is wasted when not directed away from the target. Twisting the wrist during the speed-up-and-stop on the forward cast will cause additional problems. If the leader and fly jump to the left as the cast ends, it is because the wrist twisted to the left during the speed-up-and-stop.

Incorrect: Twisting Wrist

I begin the cast with my thumb behind the rod handle from the target.

During the speed-up-and-stop for the backcast, I twist my wrist even more.

As the rod lifts line from the water, my rod hand begins twisting outward.

This causes the line to unroll outward and not directly away from the target.

I begin the forward cast. Because I have to direct the line toward the target, my wrist must now begin returning so that my thumb is behind the handle from the target. This method of casting often results in a lot of twisted line, especially with long retrieves; each time the line rolls out and then around, a partial twist is placed in it.

My wrist has returned to its starting position as the cast ends.

I begin turning my wrist back.

Incorrect: Twisting Wrist on the Sidearm Cast

Let's take a look at twisting the wrist on a sidearm cast. This is a common mistake.

I begin the cast with my thumb behind the rod handle away from the target.

This causes the rod tip to rotate around and outward.

As the speed-up-and-stop begins for the backcast, I have twisted my wrist.

The line is forced to travel out and around a wider loop.

At the end of the backcast, I have twisted my wrist well to the outside.

I have turned my wrist so that my thumb is again behind the handle away from the target.

I begin the forward cast.

Because the line has unrolled out and around on the backcast, I have to realign it for the forward cast, wasting energy.

To deliver the fly to the target, I have to twist my wrist back to the position I started in.

I have returned my rod hand to the starting position as the cast ends.

Here's a front view of the large loop formed when you twist your wrist: Twisting the wrist on the backcast causes a wide loop.

Here's the same view of a straight wrist loop. The line goes straight away from the target because of a straight wrist.

Straight Wrist (Sidearm Cast)

To prevent twisting your wrist on a sidearm cast, focus on casting with your forearm and keeping your thumb opposite the target. This sequence shows a straight wrist throughout the sidearm cast.

As you begin the cast, keep your elbow on the shelf and thumb behind the rod handle, opposite the target.

Keep a straight wrist during the speed-up-and-stop.

As you continue to lift line, keep your thumb behind the handle away from the target to prevent your wrist from twisting.

This directs all the line away from the target in a tight loop.

The wrist has not twisted as the backcast ends.

The energy of the cast in a tight loop travels directly toward the target.

When you begin the forward cast, make sure that your thumb is still behind the handle away from the target.

Because you did not twist your wrist, all energy has been directed away from and back to the target.

Speed up and stop with a straight wrist.

Elbow on the Shelf

You should rarely elevate your elbow while casting. Imagine walking up to a shelf that is as high as your elbow. During most of the casting stroke, your elbow should remain on this imaginary shelf. If you watch many great casters using either one- or two-handed rods, they keep their elbows as if they are on that shelf and change the trajectory of their casts by the direction of the rod tip and hand stop. The elbow should track along the shelf for shorter casts. But when you extend your rod hand well behind you, it is all right to raise your elbow slightly after the stop.

Raising the elbow off the shelf vertically or to the side tends to open the loop and reduces the total body movement. It forces you to use your arm and shoulder joint and less of your body to aid in long or more difficult casts. Long-time fly casters who develop rotator cuff problems almost always have been casting with their elbow raised high through the cast. With practice, you can become a good caster even if you raise your elbow on the backcast, but this stresses or tears your

rotator cuff, and since you tend to flex your wrist quite a bit, you could develop tennis elbow from casting heavier rods and flies. The higher above the imaginary shelf the elbow rises, the more the shoulder joint rotates. Keeping the elbow on the shelf and moving the body back and forth results in little or no rotation of the shoulder joint. All the energy of the cast is directed away from and back to the target, and little strength or effort is required.

On the backcast, I do not generally bend my wrist at all. I just make the whole cast with my forearm. When I come forward, I can carry my hand in a more level position so I turn my forearm and wrist over until my thumb is parallel with the water at the end of the side or vertical cast. That tilts the rod down slightly, forms a tight loop, and prevents tailing loops. That is why, on the forward cast, I raise the elbow slightly as I duck the rod tip. Taking the elbow off the shelf to accomplish this move is okay.

Elbow on the Shelf (Short Cast)

For a short cast, keep your elbow on the shelf and thumb behind the rod handle away from the target. Face the target, and distribute your weight evenly between your feet. Begin to rotate your body and your forearm back to make a short backcast.

As you make the backcast, you don't have to rotate your body very much or take your forearm back far. Just before the backcast unrolls, begin the forward cast, moving your forearm slightly forward.

Through the forward cast, focus on keeping your elbow on the shelf and not twisting your wrist. At the end of the stroke, make a brief speed-up-and-stop with minimal flexing of the wrist.

Elbow on the Shelf (Medium Cast)

Facing the target, place your elbow on the shelf and your thumb behind the rod handle, opposite the target, and distribute your weight evenly between both feet. Swivel your body slightly as your forearm moves behind you to begin the backcast. If your body and forearm make the backcast, you won't strain your rotator cuff or elbow tendons.

Continue to rotate your body back to the starting position while your forearm moves toward the target.

As your rod hand speeds up and stops, determining the angle of the backcast, your elbow is on the shelf. Rotate your chest about 45 degrees from the target, and shift your weight to the rear foot. Speed up and stop with your forearm to complete the backcast, and do not flex your wrist. Just before the backcast unrolls, begin the forward cast, using body rotation and your forearm.

As the rod reaches this position, speed up and stop, with little flexing of the wrist, to produce a tight loop. As the cast ends, you have not strained your rotator cuff, and your wrist and elbow stayed on the shelf, ensuring all energy was delivered away from and back to the target.

Elbow on the Shelf (Long Cast)

Face the target with your elbow on the shelf and thumb behind the rod handle, opposite the target.

Keep your elbow on the shelf as you sweep the rod behind you on the backcast. Use your body to help load the rod and make the cast, and swivel your body and shift your weight to your rear foot. Swiveling your body while casting with your forearm delivers a fast backcast. Keep your elbow on the shelf and thumb behind the grip, opposite the target. The angle of the backcast is determined by the angle your rod hand speeds up and stops. On a high angle cast, your elbow still remains on the shelf. This ensures all the energy flows away from the target. If your elbow rises off the shelf, the line loop opens and energy is wasted.

After you speed up and stop, you can extend your arm farther back. After a speed-up-and-stop, you can raise your elbow slightly from the shelf, and it will not affect the cast. Shift your body weight to your rear foot as your body swivels until your chest is 90 degrees from the target. On an extra-long cast, this positions the rod almost parallel to the water. Throughout the backcast, no stress is placed on the rotator cuffs, and the wrist has not bent.

Just before the backcast unrolls, begin the forward cast.

Swivel your body and bring your forearm forward to make the cast. Gradually shift your weight to your front foot.

Continue to swivel the body forward while the forearm aids in the cast, keeping your elbow on the shelf the entire time. Make a speed-up-and-stop by flexing your wrist slightly. On an extra-long cast, it is okay to slightly elevate your elbow off the shelf after the speed-up-and-stop.

Incorrect: Elbow off the Shelf

Here are some sequences where my elbow leaves the shelf.

I begin the cast with the rod low and my elbow on the shelf.

As I raise the rod to lift line from the water, my elbow begins leaving the shelf.

As I speed up and stop to begin the backcast, my elbow is off the shelf.

My rod hand is high at the end of a cast and descends, throwing the line and large loop down behind me.

Because my elbow is so far off the shelf, the rod tip travels in a circular motion and produces a wide, inefficient loop.

I begin the forward cast with my rod hand well above my head and elbow high above the shelf.

As my hand sweeps forward, my hand naturally begins to drop.

As the elbow nears the shelf, the cast ends with a large, inefficient loop.

The rod and elbow continue the circular path as they descend, causing the rod to form a large line loop.

Incorrect: Elbow off the Shelf

I begin lifting the line from the water.

As I speed up and stop to begin the backcast, my elbow is rising.

Because my elbow has risen, the rod tip travels in a curve, making a large, inefficient loop.

Because I moved my elbow from low to high, the rod is forced to throw the line around a curve.

I end the backcast with my elbow high off the shelf.

With my elbow well off the shelf, I begin the forward cast.

As the rod sweeps forward, I begin dropping my elbow.

Dropping my elbow back toward the shelf causes the rod tip to throw a large open loop.

Dropping my elbow from a high position has produced a large line loop.

Keeping the Elbow on the Shelf

Begin the cast with your elbow on the imaginary shelf. This imaginary shelf should be about as high as your elbow when it is resting on your side. Make sure your thumb is behind the handle away from the target, and your hand is held low.

Lift the line from the water and begin the speed-up-and-stop while the rod tip is still rising, with your elbow sliding back on the shelf.

When you end the speed-up-and-stop, your thumb should be opposite the target behind the rod handle, and your elbow should still be on the imaginary shelf. If so, you direct all the cast's energy away from the target in a tight loop.

When you begin the forward cast, come forward with your elbow on the shelf and the rod handle traveling straight ahead.

Continue bringing your rod hand forward with the elbow sliding on the shelf, creating a tight loop with almost all energy directed toward the target.

Keeping the Elbow on the Shelf

Begin the cast with your elbow on the imaginary shelf and thumb behind the rod handle away from the target.

Lift the rod from the water with the elbow on the shelf.

While the rod tip is still rising, speed up and stop to create the backcast.

Keep the elbow on the shelf as you direct the rod tip up and away from the target during the speed-up-and-stop, producing a nice loop.

Loop continues to unroll.

Stopping while the rod tip is rising creates a flat backcast, with most of the energy traveling away from the target.

When you begin the forward cast, slide your elbow forward on the shelf.

The rod hand moves in a straight path as your elbow stays in contact with the shelf during the speed-up-and-stop. A tight loop travels straight ahead.

Stop the rod completely after your acceleration to allow the loop to unroll well away from the tip.

Once the line loop is well away from the rod tip, you can lower the rod to the fishing position.

OTHER KEY CONCEPTS
The Grip

Gripping the fly rod is like gripping a baseball bat, golf club, or tennis racquet. If you are up at the plate and about to hit a ball, gripping the bat hard the entire time would compromise your swing, you wouldn't hit the ball very well, and your hands would hurt at the end of the day. Good hitters grip the bat just before they make contact with the ball. You don't grip your golf club hard the entire time you swing for a long drive; you grip it just before you hit the ball. When serving in tennis, you grip the racquet just as the ball makes contact with it, not through the entire swing. Instead, the club, bat, or racquet is held just firmly enough to control it through the stroke. Through the fly-casting stroke, only grip the rod hard just before you speed up and stop. Blisters or red hands at the end of a practice session or day of fishing are signs that you are gripping the rod too hard, which is common when you are trying hard to learn something.

I have found that keeping your thumb behind the target on top of the cork grip is the grip that allows you to make the best stop with the rod. I tell students to keep their thumbnails traveling back from the target and toward the target, which keeps the rod tip traveling straight. Many small-stream anglers put their pointer fingers on top of the cork, but that pointer finger is not nearly as strong as the thumb, so you can't accelerate or stop the rod as easily.

Handshake. This grip is less popular. Because the rod handle is positioned between the thumb and fingers, it may flex during the back and forward cast. Strong casters are able to hold it firmly, but many people can't, and this grip produces larger loops.

Thumb on top. If the thumb is behind the handle away from the target before beginning the back or forward cast, most of the energy is efficiently directed away from and back to the target. In this position, it is also easier to stop when using heavier rods.

Pointer finger on top. This grip is a favorite among those who fish light lines and small streams for trout. Some claim it is more accurate than the thumb-on-top grip, but I don't think that is true. Also, it is a poor grip for longer casts and heavier rods.

Drifting

Drifting with a rod is when you continue to move the rod tip after the stop, either by bringing it farther back (for the vertical cast) or extending your arm even farther behind you on a sidearm cast. If you are going to drift the rod, you have to perfect your stop. When you stop a rod, the bottom of the loop is at the tip of the rod. If you stop the rod and immediately begin to lower the rod behind or in front of you, you tear open the loop and divert energy from the cast. To drift properly, you have to learn to wait long enough to allow the loop to escape the tip so that you don't pull it down, which takes a lot of practice. Once the loop gets 10 feet or so beyond the rod, you can drift back and not affect the direction of the cast or the size of the loop. You also have to elevate the hand and arm to drift properly, and you start to get into rotator cuff problems.

Advanced casters can combine a really good stop with some drift to get the maximum rod loading. On some of my longer casts, I stop the rod dead, but then I continue to extend my arm back after giving the line a chance to clear the rod tip. The longer you can move the rod, the longer you can store energy to create higher line speed. Drifting allows the caster to accelerate the rod over a longer distance, but I think it is best for beginners to learn to stop the rod where they want to go and become proficient at that before experimenting with the drifting technique.

At times, you can also drift on the forward cast. If you need to work more line out and you want to make a long cast, pick the line up and shoot some line on the backcast. Then when you shoot line on the forward cast, if you extend the arm and rod forward at the end of that cast, you are drifting on the forward cast, and lengthening your casting stroke. This gives you more line speed on the backcast, which allows you to shoot even more line.

Force

One of the reasons that I think women learn to cast better than men is that they rarely apply too much power during the cast. Some of the worst casters that I have encountered, at least in the beginning, are big, strong people who use too much force to make the cast. When you accelerate too fast and really slam the rod, the tip tends to bob up and down, which causes shock waves. Over the years I have come to realize that calling the motion before the stop a "power stroke" implies that you have to apply power, so I instead opt to call it a speed-up-and-stop.

I used to be able to cast great distances when I was younger, but as I got into my middle and late seventies, I realized that I couldn't cast that far anymore. Up to about 90 feet, skilled technique has everything to do with how you can cast. To cast beyond that, you need strength. Two things that really

make the cast go a long distance are how fast you can accelerate the rod and how quickly you can come to a stop.

Good fly casters are constantly monitoring and regulating their line speeds as they adjust to different conditions. Sometimes you need to accelerate rapidly in the casting stroke: If you want to make a tuck or curve cast, the faster you speed up and stop, the greater the curve you are going to get in the line or the greater the line tucks under the rod tip in a tuck cast. At other times, like when making a stack cast or other dry-fly presentation, you want a relatively gentle forward cast. Knowing when to apply force and when to cast softly allows you to cast more efficiently throughout the day.

Tight, fast loops are not always the best result. They are the most efficient, but there are many times when making presentations to fish that you don't want a fast, tight loop. When dry-fly fishing, for instance, I often deliberately open my loop to not only prevent tailing loops, but also to slow down and soften the presentation of the cast. Most slack-line casts are better made with a gentle forward cast. If you make the forward cast part of a stack cast with great force, the line will sail out, get to the end, kick, and recoil back, and you'd have a terrible, uncontrolled cast. The same thing applies on a reach cast. In a good reach cast, the line travels high above the water, but very slowly, and that gives you the opportunity to lay the line to one side. If the line was traveling fast, particularly low and fast, you don't have the time to make a good reach. Another place where you would not use a high-speed line is when you want to make an aerial mend. With an aerial mend, you stop the rod high, with only enough speed to get the fly to the target. And then you decide where you want to make the mend. If you generate high line speed, you won't give the mend the time it needs to form and fall to the water.

You also don't want to use force when you are casting weighted shooting heads and sinking lines. You do move the line fast through the backcast, but the forward cast should be gentle. As we discuss in the chapter on casting weighted flies, if you come forward with too much force, the end of the sinking line tends to dump on you. It's almost like when a dog runs out of leash, the force knocks him back. If you are throwing with the wind, you need to make a tight backcast, but on your forward cast you should not apply that much force because the wind is going to carry your line. When you cast into the wind, you do the opposite, driving your forward cast toward the water with high line speed.

Trajectory

An important and often-ignored aspect of presentation is the angle at which you direct the fly line on the forward cast. Many people cast at the same angle all the time, but good cast-

> *Tight, fast loops are not always best. They are the most efficient, but there are many times when making presentations to fish that a slower, wider loop is best.*

ers modify the trajectory of the cast depending on fishing conditions. I make most of my forward casts directing the fly above eye level so that it is slightly climbing. There are two reasons for this: Weighted flies—large or small—splash too much if we direct the cast toward the water. For example, bonefish flies with lead or bead-chain eyes if directed toward the surface will hit the water so hard that most bones will spook. When casting these flies, I like to cast at an upward angle so that the climbing line spends most of its energy and lands softer. Larger flies with substantial weight, if not directed above the surface, will probably fall short of the target because frequently the angler didn't develop enough line speed on the cast. When casting in the wind, the angle at which you aim your line can make or break the cast—you should drive the line to the water when casting into a wind, but when the wind is at your back, stop the rod tip while it is climbing.

The most efficient backcast is 180 degrees from the target, so you should modify your backcast depending on the angle of your forward cast. Sometimes you have to cast at a much greater angle on the forward cast, and you can only do this effectively by coming back low on the backcast. The higher you aim on the stack cast, for instance, the more slack you will get in your line. When using a fast sinking line or lead-core shooting head, you again need to alter the casting angle. Because these lines in flight will fall faster than a floating line, you must direct the lines much higher on the forward cast. There are two advantages to this: If you throw such lines at the normal casting angle, they will fall short of the target. Directing such lines in a downward direction will increase the splashdown. Throwing the line higher means you will increase distance, and if the backcast is set up correctly, you eliminate the chance of heavy flies and/or the line hitting you or your fly rod. By making a low backcast and then directing the line at a high angle, the fly and line will travel well above you, and you can avoid being struck by the line or the fly. Other times, you want to cast low to the water, such as for the sidearm cast or a skip cast—or actually drive the cast at the water, such as when you are casting into the wind.

Accuracy is another reason to direct the line and fly upward. Good plug or spin casters make a slightly climbing cast with enough energy so that the lure could go well beyond the target. As the lure approaches the target, the plug caster slows the reel spool with his thumb and the spin caster uses his finger to feather the line to slow its flight, and stops the lure so it falls on the target. Fly fishers should do the same by making a climbing cast with the fly going well beyond the target. The line hand forms an O ring with the thumb and first finger around the line as it flows forward. When the fly is over the target, the line hand traps the line, stopping the fly.

Finally, the climbing technique helps the angler throw a tighter loop. By making a speed-up-and-stop while slightly climbing, there is less tendency to follow through after the stop and pull the loop apart.

Accuracy

Accuracy helps you catch more fish, whether casting to rising trout or hitting the holes in the lily pads when fishing popping bugs for largemouth bass. Many people think that saltwater fishing is just chuck and chance it, but good anglers can drop their flies in front of a tailing bonefish or a cruising tarpon, or direct them under overhanging mangroves to catch the snook that wait in ambush. Everything from large tarpon to small brook trout demands accuracy.

Consider a hunter who shoots a deer. The hunter does not shoot *at* the deer. He would probably miss it. Instead, he aims at a very specific area of the deer's body. So it is with accurate fly casting to small and hard-to-hit targets. The fly fisherman doesn't throw at the shoreline. The caster focuses on a very small target. When people shoot a gun, bow, or cast, they tend to instinctively hit what they focus on. Police are taught to look intently at the target, raise the pistol, and pull the trigger when they "feel" the gun is aimed properly. Instead of casting at the fish, you should concentrate on where you want to the fly to land while watching the fish in your peripheral vision.

Few fly fishermen realize that on almost every cast made with a weighted fly, they throw an inaccurate curve in the leader and fly. The line goes in the direction the rod tip speeds up and stops. If you are a right-handed caster, chances are you tilt the fly rod tip outward as you make the forward cast. When the rod tip is tilted outward on the speed-up-and-stop, the rod tip flexes to the left, causing the leader and fly to swing to the left. Of course, if you are a left-hander, the fly will curve to the right. This is the main reason why freshwater trout fishermen throw an inaccurate cast with weighted flies—especially nymphs. To make an accurate cast, the rod tip must speed up and stop in the direction of the target. You can make any kind of backcast (side, angled, or vertical), but at the finish of the forward cast, the rod must be in a vertical position so the tip can stop in line with the target.

Accuracy with spinning or plug tackle is dependent upon the angler stopping the lure's flight on target. Most fly fishermen cast at the target and then release the fly line and hope to God the fly lands where they want. But it doesn't have to be that way. You can get extreme accuracy with a fly rod if you cast the line in a slightly climbing manner with enough energy to go beyond the target. Instead of releasing the line, shoot it through an O formed with your first finger and thumb (acting like a rod guide as line flows through it), and as the fly nears the target, compress the two fingers to slow the line's flight speed. When the fly is over the target, trap the line so the fly falls where you want it.

If the line flows through your two fingers, it is also under your control at all times. If you suddenly realize the cast is going wrong, trap the line and make another backcast and forward cast. If you release the line during its flight, you have to look down to recover it after the fly lands. That means taking your eyes off the fish, which may be difficult to locate again.

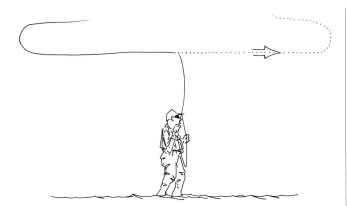

The most efficient backcast is 180 degrees from your target. If you want to direct the forward cast straight ahead, the backcast should be aligned as shown.

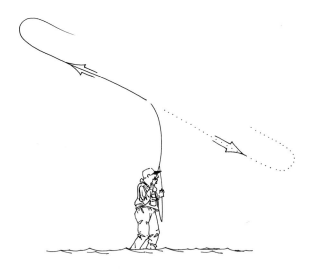

If you want to direct the forward cast downward, you need to have a high backcast so all the energy of the cast can be unrolled to the target.

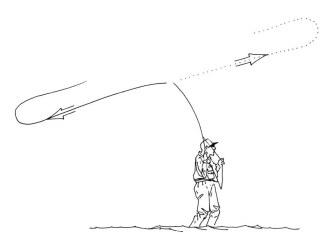

If you want a climbing forward cast, the backcast should be low and in as straight a path as possible with the forward cast.

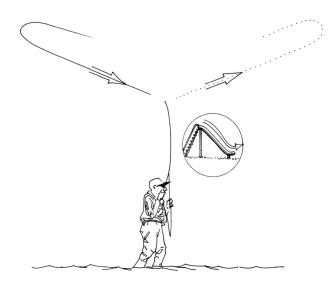

If you want a level or climbing forward cast, your backcast should not be elevated. The change in direction from a high backcast to an elevated forward cast dissipates the energy of the cast. Consider a slide on a playground: The ends of all sliding boards turn up slightly to bring the child to a safe stop. You don't want the cast to slow to a stop right in front of you—like the child on a slide—so don't dissipate its energy by changing direction abruptly.

To make an efficient roll cast (or Spey cast), you must align the backcast (or D loop) opposite the target. This allows all the energy to be directed toward the target. It is also important to tilt the rod slightly away from yourself so the drooping line clears the rod as you make the forward cast.

Shoot the line through your fingers, and you never have to take your eyes off the fish to begin retrieving. When the fly hits the water, you can either begin a retrieve or instantly set the hook. When casting for long distances where accuracy is not a consideration, the angler releases the shooting line.

If fishing conditions permit, a vertical forward cast is the most accurate. On short casts, you can make a vertical backcast and a vertical forward cast, but for longer casts, I make a sidearm backcast and come through vertically.

One of the biggest hindrances to accurate casting is when the wind blows hard from the caster's side. The cast is made, and the wind forces the line to fall well downwind of the target. To cast accurately in this situation, direct your cast downward toward the target. When the rod tip stops, the line is committed to the target. As soon as the rod tip stops, immediately put the rod tip in the water. This will place all line between the target and rod tip in or under water where the wind cannot affect it. Even in a stiff breeze, you will be able to present the fly within inches of the target.

If casting into the wind, it often helps to aim your cast at the water.

When making a stack cast, aim your cast high.

CHAPTER 3

Casting and the Body

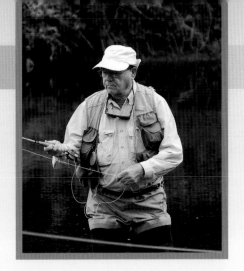

For centuries fly fishermen have been taught to cast with their arms and wrists only. Yet I cannot think of a modern sport where the best participants use only their arms and wrists. A baseball pitcher uses his entire body to hurl the ball at the catcher, as will an outfielder trying to cut off a runner from reaching home plate. Someone serving in tennis uses the entire body to drive the ball past an opponent. Golfers do the same when driving. Watch someone who throws a javelin or a discus and notice how he uses his body to compete. Even good ping-pong players use most of their bodies and arms to hit a tiny ball at incredible speeds. Yet we persist in teaching casting using almost all arm and wrist. This inefficient method prevents those who do not have powerful arms and wrists from participating in our sport. Even if they can manage on a trout stream, they cannot enjoy other aspects of our sport such as saltwater or steelhead fly fishing because they do not have the arm and wrist strength.

When wielding larger rods and throwing heavier lines and flies, using only the arm and wrist can lead to tennis elbow and torn rotator cuff. When you need to use heavier rods, lines, and flies for distance casting or battling the wind, your body should make the most of the cast by rotating or swiveling to sweep the rod back and forth during casting. When the cast is properly executed, your rotator cuffs remain immobile and little wrist action is required. This method will not rock the boat and create fish-alerting waves if your upper body swivels and you do not shift from one foot to the other.

The more effort required, the more the body swivels to aid the cast. The body can be used when making a vertical, angled, or side cast. The following photos illustrate how to use the body more to make the side cast.

Casting with the Body

Position your right foot back (if you are right-handed). The longer the cast, the wider your stance should be.

Keep your thumb behind the rod handle away from the target and your elbow on the imaginary shelf throughout the cast. Haul as you begin to pivot your body and bring your arm away from the target.

Swiveling rapidly while moving the arm back and hauling on the line loads the rod.

I am pointing at my rod hand and elbow to show that they both remain low as they travel back.

Continue to swivel your body back as you shift your weight to your rear foot. Move your hauling hand toward the rod butt.

As the backcast nears its end, swivel your body back and start to move the rod hand forward. Your hauling hand should be close to the rod butt so there is no slack as you start the forward cast.

The rod loads well as you swivel your body forward and bring your rod hand toward the target.

Because you've used your body, you can make this cast with little effort. It is important for good fishing technique to maintain the body in a vertical position while swiveling.

Incorrect Casting with the Body

This photo demonstrates how *not* to move the body when casting.

I am rocking back on the backcast, and my body has not remained vertical.

If you are in a boat—and in shallow water—if your body sways back and forth, you can rock the boat, sending small waves outward that can alert fish. Rocking the upper body tends to open loops, too.

PREVENTING SHOULDER INJURY

Dr. George W. Yu

So much of what we do on a daily basis depends on our shoulder joint. We take for granted simple things such as putting on our coats, picking up a baby, lifting groceries, reaching behind to pick up papers, or turning during sleep—until we hurt this delicate joint.

You may have a set of good chest and shoulder muscles and have a sense of strength and power, but the truth of the matter is that your entire shoulder and shoulder blade is connected to the rest of your body by one little collarbone called "clavicle" and four muscles called "rotator cuff." Downstream, there is another muscle attachment from the arm bone—humerus—to the chest and back called the "lats, pecs, and deltoids." On a relative scale, the shoulder joint is more fragile and delicate compared to the larger joints such as the hips to legs and the pelvis to the back.

A severe fracture of the collarbone can immobilize the entire shoulder.

WHEN DO WE GET HURT?

For most fly fishermen and sportsmen, the shoulder takes a beating from the following:

- Weekend Warrior Syndrome of overachievers who are not in top physical condition.
- Repetitive use of the same motion of the shoulder, such as in serving in tennis, casting a 10-weight fly rod, hitting golf balls at the driving range, etc.
- Sleeping in strained positions such as arms behind your head and awaking in pain is more common than we think.
- Sudden vigorous exercise of aging atrophied joint ligaments ("ligamentosis") and frail muscle tendons ("tendonosis") often seen in elderly people with hormone decline: andropause and menopause.
- Poor nutritional support to maintain thick and long tendons of muscles, and thick ligaments to bones for stability.
- Impact or contact injuries from falling off a horse, bicycle, motorcycle, or an automotive accident with a contusion of the shoulder.

BASIC ANATOMY

We need to define what it means when we talk about any joint. The example in figure 1 shows how two bones are surrounded or enveloped by muscle groups that contract and result in flexion, extension, and torque rotation

Ligaments are what hold bones together to stabilize the joint in place. To use a building analogy, the ligaments are the bolts holding two frames together as the internal structure, and the outer layer of the drywall, brick, or wood covering over the frame are the "muscles" attached to the frame.

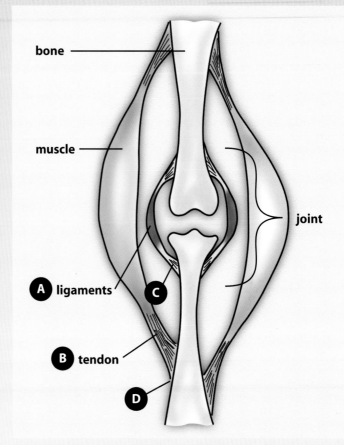

Fig. 1. A: Ligaments hold bone to bone. **B:** Tendons hold muscle to bone. **C:** Site of ligament tear. **D:** Site of tendon tear.

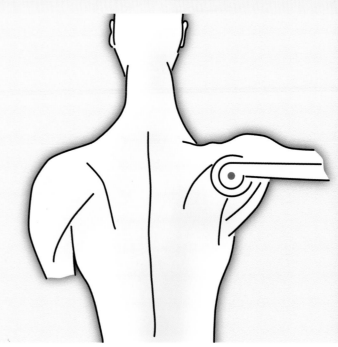

Fig. 2. Ligaments are like bolts holding moving bone parts together. Sometimes they can loosen with overuse.

Preventing Shoulder Injury continued

The blood circulation to these areas of the ligaments is sparse, and the most common site of injury is at the junction or connection between the bone and ligament (see figure 1, C). These areas of injury are slow to heal, as seen in a sprained ankle, which heals slower than fractured or broken leg bones.

Muscle and tendons are the secondary structures that support the ligaments and create movements. Tendons are the end pieces of muscle that attach to the bone and are susceptible to injury at the attachment to the bone (see figure 1, D). The tendon attachment to bone is also an area of poor circulation and is therefore slow to heal when torn. When a whole tendon or

whole ligament is torn, you can hear the "pop" when the accident occurs.

The composite of two bones and the ligaments and space in between are what make up a joint in the most simplified model.

When ligaments are injured, the muscles must contract to hold the joint in "painless" positions, which then leads to muscle overstrain and spasms and a second level of pain. If the injury is neglected for a longer period of time, from several months to years, these pain reflexes can cascade and become so severe that even the skin and fat underneath the injured joints can be tender to touch and painful. Massage, acupuncture, myofascial injections into muscles, and neural therapy all relax the muscle groups in abnormal contractions and attempt to balance the opposing muscle groups, which perform either flexions or extensions.

In sports the most common injuries occur at points C and D in figure 1.

SHOULDER ANATOMY

Four muscles with three supporting muscles keep the shoulder "connected" to the chest. The clavicle, or collarbone, is the only structure holding the entire shoulder complex to the rest of the body. The shoulder has numerous ligaments important to the surgeon, but of only academic interest for the layman. However, for the sportsman and doctor it is important to understand the four-muscle group called the "rotator cuff,"

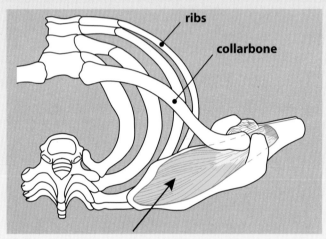

Fig. 3.

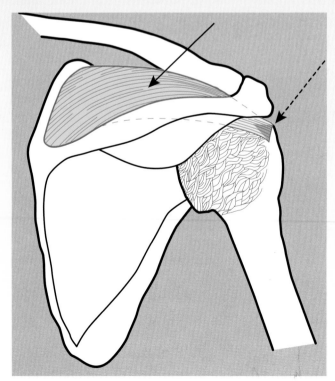

Fig. 4. The top and back views of the shoulder show the supraspinatus muscle.

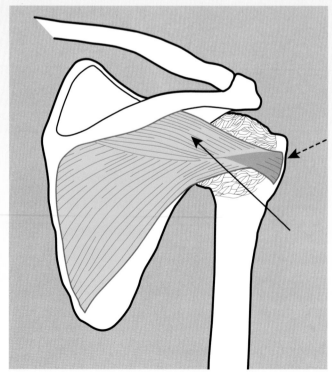

Fig. 5. The back view of the shoulder shows the infraspinatus muscle.

which has tendons attached to the shoulder and arm bones and surrounds the shoulder socket. The illustrations show each muscle and tendon attachment. The top muscle is the supraspinatus (figures 3 and 4), the bottom muscle is the infraspinatus (figure 5), the inside front muscle is the subscapularis (figure 6), and the last is the teres minor (figure 7). Injury or "tear" of the rotator cuff usually involves the tendon attachment to the arm.

Teres major, latissimus dorsi (better known as "lats"), pectoralis (better known as "pecs"), and deltoid muscles are big supporting muscles that keep the connectiveness of arms and shoulder to the rest of the chest in all sports activities. The muscle is resilient to injury and heals quickly, but the tendons on either end of the muscle are fragile and heal slowly.

It is usually the tendons that become inflamed or injured from overuse, in impact collision injury, or entrapment. Especially in the older sportsman, there is usually a thinning of the ligaments and tendons as well as muscle bodies due to male hormone decline, andropause, that makes these individuals more susceptible to injury.

Once the injury has occurred, the healing process is slow in all tendons (and ligaments) because the blood and lymphatic circulations to these areas are poor compared to muscle tissues.

If the injury is long-standing, there is also a tendency to waste away as an atrophic process called "tendonosis" for tendon attachments to bone and "ligamentosis" for ligaments attached to the bones.

EFFICIENT MUSCLE GROUP MOVEMENT

When we talk about "connectiveness" between arms and body to generate maximum power and smoothness of movements, we are talking about muscle groups working together as one piece. In golf, tennis, fly fishing, martial arts, and boxing, the principles are the same. The famous golf legend Jimmy Ballard wrote a book called *How to Perfect Your Golf Swing Using Connection*, which makes the point of connecting the shoulder with the chest muscle to create a perfect swing. But more than a perfect swing, that same connection protects the rotator cuff from overuse and injury. Connection of and contracted arm and shoulder muscle groups together at the moment of impact are the best and most efficient motion to avoid injury. When you perform a swing or a cast as "one-piece motion" by using two or more muscle groups together, you generate more power with less strain on each group. Another way of saying it is if two muscle groups are contracting and moving too far apart or separately from each other, there will be more strain on each group of muscles and less net power. This "disconnection" of muscle groups also increases the risk of tendon and ligament injury at the bony attachments. Pilates exercise connects internal muscles and ligaments of the upper and lower body to maintain the most efficient postures and motions with the least strain on the body. This will be illustrated when we see Lefty's

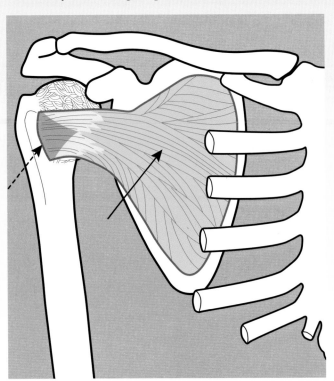

Fig. 6. The front view of the shoulder shows the subscapularis muscle.

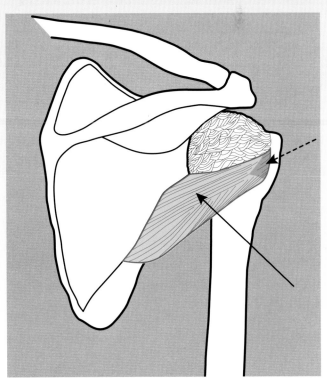

Fig. 7. This back view of the shoulder shows the teres minor muscle.

Preventing Shoulder Injury continued

fly-casting efficiency with heavier saltwater rods. Using 9- and 10-weight saltwater rods and reels, the enthusiastic fisherman cannot just use his arms alone for repeated casting, but must incorporate the chest, shoulders, hips, and legs and release the power generated to the extended arm.

The following serial photographs illustrate the efficiency of two large groups of connected muscle groups: the first, upper legs and hips, and the second group of connected muscle group around the shoulder to the chest.

Efficient Casting Motions Using Heavy Saltwater Rods between 9-weight and 12-weight

Lefty poses as a right-handed person, starting with the right foot behind the left.

In the backcast, the body weight is shifted to the back right leg and foot. The chest and shoulder muscle are connected as one piece. The most common problem is an incomplete backcast that then sets up for a poor forward cast. The frustrated angler will pound his arms to death and injure himself trying to make the perfect forward cast.

At the end of the backcast, Lefty's elbow is not far from his chest to keep the "connectiveness."

At the beginning of the forward cast, his shoulder and arm are one piece, and both muscle groups are contracted together. Notice that the lower group of muscle of the hips and leg have shifted the weight forward.

At the same time, the upper muscle group of the arm and shoulder has shifted the weight forward, thereby transferring the power and inertia to the arms and hand during the release phase of the cast.

All muscle groups are interconnected in this casting motion. The big muscle groups of the legs and pelvis have connected to the arm and shoulder to the chest to create a powerful cast without straining individual muscle groups such as the rotator cuff alone.

WHAT TO DO IMMEDIATELY AFTER AN INJURY

- Ice pack to the shoulder to cool the inflammation.
- Aspirin, anti-inflammatory medications such as Motrin, and even pain medications such as Percocet 10/325 milligrams or Demerol 50 milligrams every six hours as needed.
- Local acupuncture to give immediate relief pain and decrease swelling.
- Resting the shoulder also means sleeping with arm and shoulder close to the chest. Wearing a T-shirt over the shoulder or tying the arm loosely to the chest and abdomen before going to sleep helps to prevent further injury.

WHAT TO DO IF IT DOES NOT GET BETTER ONE MONTH AFTER THE INJURY

The more common and serious shoulder injury problems are chronic sufferers. Most of the people in this category have already gone through the "physical therapy and medication" routine and still are having problems in their daily activity. Many are professional athletes who cannot perform their best and complain of pain awakening their sleep. I suggest the following sequence of treatments that have been the most useful:

MRI radiological study can define the soft tissues of the four-muscle group and tendon injury. If there is a "complete" (through-and-through) tear of the one of the tendons, only a surgical repair will correct the problem. For partial tears, many options are possible for the healing.

For muscle with tendon injury, a combination of acupuncture of muscle and myofascial injection therapy have been very helpful (pioneered by the late Dr. Janet Travell, the physician for John F. Kennedy).

Partial tears or injuries to tendons and ligament attachments to the bony surface will heal slowly, and many already have atrophied ligaments and tendons (ligamentosis and tendosis); these people should consider proliferative therapy or prolotherapy, which is an injection treatment using dextrose 12 percent with an anesthetic such as lidocaine or procaine to the area ligament or tendon attachments to bone. This treatment has been successful with few side effects. Recently there has been publicity on this simple form of treatment. Bode Miller, the American Olympic skier, has used this treatment for his knee injury successfully. Though not fully understood,

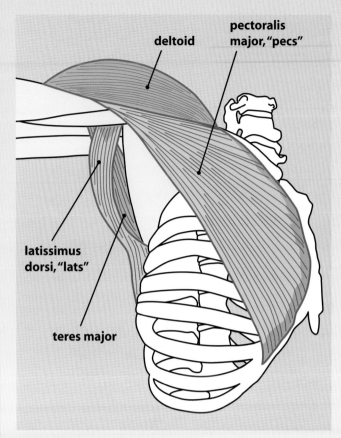

Supporting muscles for connectiveness.

the research team at University of Wisconsin with National Institute of Health funding has taken a major initiative to study the mechanism of ligament growth after treatment.

Nutritional supplementation with Knox gelatin and vitamin C was used in the past by women to harden and to beautify fingernails and toenails (before artificial nails), but the same substances, procollagen and collagen, will strengthen and rebuild all connective tissues as well as skin, nails, ligaments, and tendons. Many of the patients with musculoskeletal pains have recovered completely with long-term use of this supplement after 2 to 3 months. Knox gelatin, ½ cup a day, with glucosamine sulfate (derived from powdered shrimp shell and crab shell) work together for a good combination, and Vitamin C should also be taken with this combination, 3 grams a day. MSM supplements also help the healing process. The use of fish oil on a daily basis will prevent and lessen inflammation of all body tissues.

Using the shoulder joint efficiently and performing daily exercises are imperative to healing. I cannot overstress the need to cross-train for any athlete who specializes in one sport, such as fly fishing. Cross-training means playing different sports or going to the weight room to exercise muscles and tendons that are underutilized in your favorite sport. This training keeps the opposing muscle groups balanced. Overuse

Preventing Shoulder Injury continued

Keeping the shoulder in tip-top form.

of one set of muscles always result in weakening of opposing muscles and tendons, thus creating imbalance and more chances of injury at the joint. In addition, jumping jacks, jumping rope, push-ups, and chin-ups are great ways to strengthen the shoulder. I especially like the easy technique of the "coin rotation" of the shoulder joint. This exercise, which consists of rotating your outstretched arms and index finger around an imaginary 25-cent circle using only shoulder muscles, is easy and convenient for the busy person.

Improper arm position during sleep is a common way to reinjure a healing shoulder joint. Many sleep studies have demonstrated all kinds of shoulder positions, and you can easily do the same if your spouse stays awake to take serial pictures of your arm and shoulder positions while you sleep. Lefty, being very resourceful, uses a side barrier to prevent the arms and shoulders from getting behind the head. You can create your own ways to avoid sleep position injuries, such as wearing a T-shirt over the injured shoulder or even tying a strap to prevent excessive arm extension during unconscious sleep.

If you understand how to protect your delicate shoulder joint, learn the most efficient casting methods, and use simple remedies to strengthen your injured shoulder, then you will have many years of casting to the big one. Stay healthy, eat well, and cherish that special joint. Good casting and tight lines.

CASTING WITHOUT ROTATOR CUFF

If you elevate your elbow on the backcast and lower it on the forward cast, you strain your rotator cuff. The heavier the rod, the more air-resistant the fly, and the longer the distance you try to obtain, the greater the danger of developing a torn rotator cuff. Young or strong anglers may not have a problem now, but they tend to develop this painful problem later in life. For people who are not young or strong, the likelihood of developing a torn rotator cuff is highly possible when they use tackle that is a bit heavy for them, or they are trying to cast far distances. Using your whole body to help cast places less strain on the arm, elbow, and rotator cuff.

> *Reduce the likelihood of getting tennis elbow by rotating your body during the cast and using your forearm more than your wrist.*

If you suffer from a torn rotator cuff or tennis elbow, I teach two methods that might allow you to cast. Several doctors have told me that torn rotator cuff problems usually occur with fly fishermen mainly from raising and lower the elbow during casting. The higher the hand and elbow rise on a back or forward cast, the greater the strain placed on the rotator cuffs. By keeping the elbow lower (near its normal resting position), rotating the upper body, and using just a little forearm motion during the cast, you can avoid rotator cuff problems. I am over eighty years old and have never had rotator cuff problems caused by fly casting, despite casting huge flies and heavy line for years.

Tennis elbow is caused by excessively using the wrist during casting, which causes a constant flexing of the tendons attached to the wrist and elbow. You can feel them by pressing your first two fingers just forward of the elbow joint while flexing the wrist; the tendons stretch and relax with every wrist flex. Think about how many times a fly fisherman does that in his life, especially when using the wrist to throw heavy lines and flies.

Casting Without Rotator Cuff

Footwork is important when using this technique. A right-hander should place the right foot to the rear; a left-hander, the opposite. For a short cast, the foot need only be a little to the rear. The longer the cast, the farther back you should position your foot. This allows your body to pivot during casting. Lower the rod before casting. Lock your arm firmly against your body and do not move your wrist during the cast. If your arm leaves your body, you'll aggravate the damaged rotator cuff, and if you move your wrist, you'll aggravate the tennis elbow.

Raise the rod to lift the line free of the water. Double hauling helps.

As you raise the rod, begin to shift your weight to the rear foot as your body begins to pivot. Your elbow should stay on the imaginary shelf; keep your thumb opposite the target, and begin moving your forearm and rod in concert with the pivoting body.

When the line end leaves the water, make the backcast by pivoting quickly.

Make the speed-up-and-stop by accelerating your body as you pivot it, and move your forearm back while staying on the imaginary shelf and adding a short haul so a tight loop backcast develops. Most of the weight has shifted to your rear foot. During the entire backcast, your elbow has stayed on the shelf as your forearm sweeps the rod to the rear. Your wrist is barely flexed. Note that your shoulder joint is stationary and you use your body to make the cast. No strain has been placed on the rotator cuff. To make the backcast, swivel the body and at the same time make a long single haul.

To extend the rod farther back, rotate your body farther while you move your forearm along the shelf. Almost all the weight is on your rear foot.

At the end of the cast, your body has pivoted well to the rear, and your hauling hand has moved in front of the rod butt.

Let the backcast unroll. At the end of the cast, your body should be turned well to the rear, with the rod ending well behind you.

Just before the line unrolls, begin quickly pivoting your body back and move your forearm forward along the shelf. To make the forward cast, swivel your body back to the starting position—while hauling the entire time.

Your forearm and elbow move forward on the shelf, and your wrist remains straight as your body pivots, loading the rod.

Your shoulder has not been involved and remains stationary throughout the cast as you haul on the line. With a slight flexing of the wrist, speed up and stop in the direction of the target.

As the line is unrolling, slowly lower the rod. Your body is now in the same position as at the beginning of the cast.

The rod continues to follow the fly down to the water.

There has been no strain on the rotator cuff (which remained stationary throughout the cast), and with only a slight flexing of your wrist on the final speed-up-and-stop, tennis elbow is not a problem.

In the above cast, my elbow is way off the shelf. Raising my arm like this stresses and even tears the rotator cuff over time, and takes more energy to cast heavy rods all day.

Part II

BASIC CASTS
and Techniques

CHAPTER 4

Sidearm and Overhead Casts

If you fish for different species or fish different waters, you have to adjust your tackle and technique. One day you may be casting near-weightless trout flies; the following week, air-resistant deer-hair bass bugs. On trout streams, short, accurate casts may be required one moment, but then the breeze kicks up, and you need to punch your casts into the wind to a fish feeding on the far end of the river. You may be on a guided trip, and one minute your guide rows you close to a pod of rising fish where distance isn't nearly as important as accuracy; on the way to the launch at dusk, he has you throwing large streamers with sinking lines against the bank for the river's large brown trout. If you learn to cast only one way, you limit both how you can fly-fish and what you can catch.

I don't believe that anyone should have a style of casting. My idea of a style is that you are making a repetitive motion. If you can only cast sideways, angled, or vertical, then you can only fish those ways. It has often been said that I have a side or sidearm style of casting, but if I was casting a dry fly, I wouldn't think of casting sideways, I'd make a vertical cast because that is most accurate. I may make a side cast on the backcast and a vertical on the forward. Or a vertical backcast and a vertical forward cast if I was fishing in a confined situation. I don't think you should have a rote method of casting or subscribe to a particular school of casting. A good fly fisherman can fish lots of situations under a wide variety of conditions and with a range of tackle—from light trout rods to tarpon rods. He has no style—he just has the ability to make efficient casts as the fishing conditions permit.

It's important to be able to cast many different ways so that you can effectively fish under different situations. Casting to the side and casting vertically represent extremes. I will show these methods first, because this is how most casters commonly learn. I teach the sidearm method to my students

first because I want them to be able to see what the rod and line are doing during the cast, but many instructors teach the vertical method.

For each of these sequences, I will show a wide-angle side view so that you can get an idea of the overall path of the line in relation to the body motions. Then we will zoom in for a closer look at the hand motions, and then change angles for a front view of each cast. I think it is important to show many different views of a cast so that you can get a better idea of what is taking place in the cast. I cover vertical (along with an analysis of follow-through), sidearm, 45 degree, and then the cross-arm cast.

In some of these sequences I am hauling—if you do not yet know how to haul, follow along anyway, and after spending some time with the chapter on hauling, you can come back. But the rod motions are the same regardless of whether you haul. Even when I am casting moderate distances, I often haul, and you probably will too once you read, study, and practice the techniques in chapter 5. I recommend that you, like I did, learn the basic casting motions first, get them down well, and then start introducing the haul into your repertoire.

SIDEARM CAST

I use a sidearm cast in many situations, from making stack casts and reach casts to casting shooting heads. It is invaluable and is the only way you can cast low to the water to get your fly under an obstruction or to prevent spooking fish. One of the most critical times that I use a sidearm cast, however, is when I want to pick up a long line.

Anglers usually add more force to the cast when they try to lift a long line to make a backcast. They generally raise the rod vertically to get the line off the water and make the cast. Only so much line can be lifted vertically. With the extra force applied during the speed-up-and-stop, the tip invariably dips downward. This creates sag—often deep—that must be removed before a forward cast can start. If you observe almost anyone picking up a long line with the rod lifting vertically, there will be a sag in the backcast, usually accompanied by a larger than desired loop.

There are two reasons why using a sidearm cast to pick up a long line is more efficient than a vertical cast. First, once the rod reaches a vertical position, it can no longer lift line from the surface, and the most efficient cast has all line off the surface before beginning the backcast. But with a sidearm cast, the rod continues to moves back and is able to lift considerably more line from the surface before the cast is made. Second, if the rod tip stops while it is rising on the backcast, there will be no sag. A sag occurs in the line on a backcast when the rod tip speeds up and stops while going down and back. With a sidearm cast, the angler can stop while the rod is rising.

A sidearm cast allows you to move the rod farther back, enabling you to load the rod deeper.

The side cast allows the angler to position the rod well behind and is useful for many reasons. The longer the forward stroke, the greater the potential for increasing line speed. The longer stroke increases the loading of the rod—storing extra energy for the forward cast. It also lets the angler throw a slower, more delicate forward cast and make fishing casts that are simply not possible from a vertical rod angle.

Perhaps the greatest asset of a side cast is that it reduces the chances of getting a tennis elbow or torn rotator cuff, two painful problems that often occur when 8-weight or larger rods are used repeatedly to obtain distance and throw heavier lines and flies. During the vertical stroke, the angler flexes the wrist to help propel the line back and forth. The total length of the stroke is relatively short: stopping the rod at just past vertical and often beginning the forward stroke from near that position. Because the rod moves such a short distance, the angler must use power to generate line speed. To generate this power, rotator cuffs are stressed with each back and forth motion. Every time he flexes his wrist, there is a strain on the tendons attached at the elbow. In time, the rotator cuffs are often torn and/or tennis elbow develops. Almost all serious fly fishermen who use heavier rods and lines and throwing frequently at a distance have complained about either a torn rotator cuff or tennis elbow or both. Neither of these painful experiences is necessary if the angler brings the rod sideways well to the rear before starting the forward cast. If performed correctly, there is virtually no movement to the rotator cuffs or strain on the tendons attached to the elbow. Instead the cast is made with the body rather than just the wrist and arm. Learn this technique and you will reduce your chances of suffering from torn rotator cuffs or tennis elbow.

Sidearm Cast

Begin the cast with the rod pointed at the fly and all slack removed. Tilt your rod at an angle, making sure that your thumb is opposite the target behind the grip. Begin to bring the rod back to your side.

As you take the rod back and up, begin hauling with your line hand. Watch the line and do not make the backcast until you lift all of it from the surface.

This photo demonstrates an important feature of how to avoid a sag in the line on the backcast. The rod tip should be lower than your head as it passes beyond your body so that it can stop while rising, which eliminates sag. Your upper body begins to swivel to aid in casting.

Do not lift line vertically after the rod passes beyond you. With a sidearm cast, though, you can lift the line much farther back. Haul with your line hand during the entire period, and as soon as the line end leaves the water, speed up and stop with the tip rising on the stop. To make a long and efficient backcast, pivot your body and shift your weight to your back foot to aid the cast. If you need to make a longer forward casting stroke, let your arm drift farther back. It can rise slightly from the shelf at the very end of the stroke.

Just before the loop unrolls, begin the forward cast with the rod well behind your body.

Pivot your body back, aiding the cast as your elbow slides forward on the shelf while your arm accelerates forward and your line hand is hauling.

Before making the speed-up-and-stop, the rod has traveled a long distance. The longer the stroke, the more the rod can accelerate the line and deeper it can bend it. A brief speed-up-and-stop produces a tight loop directing all the energy at the target.

Do not lower the rod until the line is unrolling.

Just before the line unrolls, lower the rod.

The cast is completed.

Close-up of the Sidearm Cast

Begin the sidearm cast with your thumb behind the handle of the rod opposite the target, elbow on the shelf, and rod hand low. The rod hand should not be much higher than the elbow for best results. If the rod hand is held too high, there is a tendency for the rod to dip downward on the backcast.

Slide your elbow along the shelf and keep your thumb behind the handle as you lift the line from the surface. Your haul should mirror the length of the rod hand's acceleration.

As soon as the line end leaves the water, speed up and stop with your rod hand and haul simultaneously. The angle of the rod has been rising throughout the backcast. It is important that the rod tip not be higher than your head, though, so that the tip can stop while still rising, creating a flat, rising backcast.

Shift your body weight to your rear foot. If you need a longer forward stroke after the speed-up-and-stop, slide your elbow back as the rod hand drifts farther to the rear.

Begin the forward cast just before the line completely unrolls.

Pivot your body and transfer your weight to the forward foot. Your elbow tracks along the shelf with your thumb behind the handle away from the target.

Simultaneously speed up and stop with your rod hand while hauling with your line hand.

Front View of the Sidearm Cast

Begin with your right foot back, your elbow on the imaginary shelf, and the rod tip near the surface.

To make a good backcast, the line should travel directly away from the target. The rod tip should stop while it is rising to ensure a flat, straight backcast line. To accomplish this, lay the rod over at 45 to 90 degrees from the body. Doing so also permits you to lift a longer line from the water than possible with a vertical lifting of the fly rod.

Use your body to help you make this cast. Keep your elbow on the shelf and thumb behind the rod handle away from the target. Do not flex your wrist on the backcast. Swivel your body, and if you move your elbow back along the shelf, rotator cuffs or the tendons at the elbow do not move. Hauling helps, especially on longer casts.

You are making most of the cast with your body, eliminating torn rotators and tennis elbow. If you need to make a much longer cast, put your right foot farther back and extend your forearm back farther.

Allow the backcast to travel to the rear.

With a short cast, as shown here, you only need to swivel the body slightly as your forearm moves forward, with your elbow staying in contact with the shelf. Your body would have swiveled farther to the rear and back again for a longer cast.

If I raise my elbow off the shelf during the back or forward cast, I will open the loop. A tight loop results if your elbow tracks back and forth on the shelf. On a cast where your arm is fully extended on the back or forward cast, it is okay to raise your elbow slightly after the speed-up-and-stop.

Lower the rod to a fishing position when the loop is well away from it.

OVERHEAD CAST

Most fly fishers are taught this cast first, and it is the most accurate short-range cast. The energy of the back and forward cast is directly away from and back to the target. For longer casts, this requires much more effort. The overhead cast brings the rod vertically forward toward the target, ensuring the line and fly are directed there. A tilted or side cast with any weighted line or fly at the end of the cast tends to hook to one side or throw a curve in the final presentation.

The best angle for accuracy is a vertical cast, bringing your arm straight back and forth from the target.

I include two sequences of a cast that, at first, look similar, but there are some subtle differences in the follow-through after my stop on the forward cast that has bearing on some of the differences between fishing casts (casts that perform well on-stream) and casting casts (casts that look good in the parking lot).

In the first sequence, I stop the rod and follow through more after the stop to slightly open the loop. When casting dry flies, you do not want high line speed all the time. The loop is still plenty tight, and efficient, but opening the loop slightly after the stop prevents tailing loops and softens the speed of the fly, which most often lends itself to better presentations for trout—when this cast is most often used. Comparing the sequences may also be helpful to see the difference between a medium-size loop (in the second sequence) and a relatively tight loop in the first sequence.

Overhead Cast

Begin the cast with the rod tip close to the surface, pointed directly at the target.

Raise the rod vertically, lifting the line.

Do not begin the backcast until you have lifted the line free from the water. With only the leader and fly in the water, begin the backcast while the rod tip is still rising.

Direct the backcast up and away from the target.

Stop the rod just past vertical as the backcast unrolls away from the target.

Just before the line unrolls, begin the forward cast.

Aim the forward cast toward the target.

Direct the cast above the target, allowing for a quieter presentation. Throughout the cast, the rod moves vertically back and forth in line with the target.

As the loop unrolls, begin to drop the rod tip.

Continue to drop the rod tip, and lower your rod hand to your side.

The cast ends.

No Follow-through

In the second sequence, when I stop the rod, I do not follow through until the line has almost unrolled. Then I drop the rod tip. This cast makes for a better looking loop and has the amount of pause that you would want if you were false casting—where you would want the line to almost unroll before beginning your backcast—but for a fishing presentation, it helps straighten out the leader, which is not always desirable, especially for slack-line presentations for trout.

Begin the cast with the rod low and all slack removed.

Raise the rod to lift the line from the water.

When the line is out of the water, make the backcast while the rod tip is still rising.

Keep your elbow on the shelf during the cast.

A short speed-up-and-stop with little or no flexing of your wrist produces a nice loop.

The loop continues to unroll.

Start the forward cast just before the line unrolls.

As the rod hand moves forward, keep your elbow on the shelf.

Direct the rod ahead during the speed-up-and-stop.

A tight loop develops because you flexed your wrist only slightly during the short speed-up-and-stop.

The loop continues to unroll.

The loop unrolls almost all the way.

Lower the rod as the line nears the target.

The cast is completed.

Side View of the Overhead Cast

Here is a close-up of the hand and arm motions for the basic vertical cast. With a vertical cast, unless the rod is drifted to the rear after the speed-up-and-stop, most of the rod loads only in the tip section for the forward cast.

Begin with your elbow on the shelf, thumb behind rod handle, and the rod aimed in the target's direction.

Raise the rod and draw the line toward you.

When the line end leaves the water, make the backcast with your forearm using little or no wrist. This ensures a tighter loop. If you need to open up the loop, then you can use some wrist motion.

For a short cast, your hand needs to travel only this far back before making a forward cast.

Front View of the Overhead Cast

This front view shows the hand and arm motions for the basic vertical cast.

Point the rod low toward the target.

Begin raising the rod to draw the line nearer while keeping your elbow on the shelf and your thumb behind the rod handle away from the target.

Continue to raise the rod tip.

When the line end leaves the water, make the backcast while the tip is still rising.

Allow the backcast to almost unroll behind you.

Begin the forward cast. Concentrate on speeding up and stopping in the direction of the target.

Note how your elbow has stayed on the shelf and your thumb is behind the handle away from the target. A short speed-up-and-stop in the final moment of the cast produces a tight loop. Allow the loop to unroll.

Do not lower the rod tip immediately after the speed-up-and-stop if you want a tight loop. Just before the loop unrolls, lower the rod to a fishing position.

45-DEGREE ANGLE

For me, an angle between 45 and 60 degrees from vertical is the most comfortable and natural arm angle. My arm is angled enough so that I can extend it, but my range of motion is not limited by taking the rod directly back and forward completely vertically. You can keep the elbow on the shelf and your thumb behind the target (you don't need to twist your wrist) anywhere from 45 to 90 degrees. Your thumb and hand can track directly away from the target so that you are unrolling the line directly away from the target. When a vertical or side backcast is not needed, a 45-degree angle is one of the most pleasant casts, requiring little effort. The longer the cast, the more your body should swivel and the farther you should pull your arm back.

45-Degree Angle

Lower the rod and face the target with your thumb behind the rod handle away from the target and your elbow on the imaginary shelf.

Angle the rod at about 45 degrees. Lift the line from the water.

Before making a backcast, make sure that you remove all the line from the water.

Swivel your body and extend your arm while hauling on the line.

With a brief speed-up-and-stop while the rod tip is rising, a tight loop forms on the backcast. Note how your body swivels and your arm travels to the rear. The longer the cast, the more your body swivels and the farther back you take your rod hand.

Allow the line to unroll.

Just before the line unrolls, begin the forward cast. Begin turning your body back toward the target, and keep your thumb behind the handle away from the target and your elbow on the shelf, and then begin to haul.

A short, fast speed-up-and-stop creates a tight loop.

This photo may appear to be a tailing loop, but it is not. It seems that way because the line loop is angled toward us on the 45-degree cast.

Because your elbow stayed on the shelf, your thumb remained behind the handle away from the target, and the speed-up-and-stop was brief, a tight loop caused all of the energy of the cast to travel toward the target.

As the cast nears the end, gradually lower the rod.

The line drops on target.

Side View of the 45-Degree Angle

Here is a close-up version of the 45-degree angle, from the beginning of the cast to the stop at the backcast.

Begin with your elbow on the shelf, thumb behind the handle away from the target, and the rod lowered.

Lift the rod directly away from the target.

When line end leaves the water and while the rod tip is still rising, make the backcast.

For a medium cast, bring the rod back only this far before making the forward cast.

Front View of the 45-Degree Angle

Tilt the rod outward at about 45 degrees. Begin the backcast with the rod low, your elbow on the imaginary shelf, and your thumb behind the rod handle away from the target. On this cast, the higher the rod tip starts above the water, the more difficult it is to make the speed-up-and-stop while the tip is rising so that a tight loop is created and all energy is directed away from the target.

Raise the rod, and when the line end leaves the water, make the backcast.

After accelerating the rod to the rear, make a short, quick speed-up-and-stop as the rod tip is rising.

After the stop, the backcast loop forms and starts to unroll.

Note that your thumb remains behind the rod handle away from the target, and your elbow stays on the shelf.

Because you did not twist your rod hand during the backcast but kept your thumb behind the rod handle away from the target, the line travels straight back. If you had twisted your wrist, the line would flow outward in a wide loop—wasting energy.

Make the forward cast with your thumb still behind the handle away from the target and your elbow on the shelf.

Make a short speed-up-and-stop of the rod tip in the target's direction, producing a tight loop. Note that throughout the cast the rod maintained the same angle. Allow the loop to travel well away from the rod.

When the unrolling loop nears the target, lower the rod tip to a fishing position.

45-Degree Angle (Longer Cast)

The 45-degree angle also allows you to make a longer cast because you can move the rod and arm back farther. This is not a very long cast, probably average fishing distances of 50 to 60 feet with the leader, but it is effortless.

The cast starts with the rod tip low. The longer the cast, the easier it is to make, if considerable line is picked up. A short line will require a series of false casts.

Continue to lift line.

Lift all line before backcasting.

Take the rod back, and angle and begin the backcast as soon as the line leaves the water. Haul during the length of the rod hand's acceleration. Your arm travels a short distance behind you. The speed-up-and-stop occurs. If the tip stopped while it was rising, a small loop causes the line to unroll straight away from the target.

The tight loop unrolls.

The loop continues to unroll.

Just before the line unrolls, begin the forward cast.

Your elbow has remained on the imaginary shelf and your thumb behind your rod hand away from the target.

Haul during the forward acceleration of the rod. Briefly speed up and stop above the target.

A nice tight loop. Because of the brief speed-up-and-stop with the tip stopping straight ahead, a taut line with a small loop is delivering all the energy of the cast toward the target.

The loop is allowed to unroll well away from the rod tip.

At this point in the cast, start to lower the rod.

Continue to lower it.

Continue to slowly lower the rod. The line continues to straighten and fall to the water. The cast ends with a soft presentation.

Cross-Shoulder Cast

The cross-shoulder cast restricts the body's movements and is usually only effective at relatively short distances. It is often used when the wind is blowing toward the casting arm side of the angler. For longer and accurate casts, see casting when wind is on the angler's side (page 291).

Make the backcast with your elbow kept low and thumb behind the rod handle away from the target. There is a tendency to elevate your rod hand, but this diverts some of the energy and often results in a large loop and poor cast.

Tilt the rod tip slightly away from you to prevent hitting yourself with the line.

When you have lifted the line end from the surface, make the backcast. Concentrate on making a short speed-up-and-stop. People tend to cast wide loops at this angle.

At the end of the backcast, make sure your elbow has remained low and that your thumb stays behind the rod handle.

Begin a normal forward cast.

Concentrate on making a short speed-up-and-stop and do not drop the rod tip immediately to prevent casting wide loops.

Allow the line loop to unroll well away from the tip. When the loop nears the target, lower the rod to a fishing position.

Side view of the cross-shoulder cast.

CHANGING ANGLES

Keeping the principles in mind, you can adjust the angle at which you cast, and even change angles on your back and forward casts to solve fly-casting problems. I cover four basic angles here—sidearm, 45 degree, vertical, and cross shoulder—but you can cast in the entire range of movement. You can make a sidearm backcast and then come forward vertically, which is what I often do on a stack cast or when casting shooting heads. The back and forward casts are subject to the basic principles of fly casting, but it may be necessary to make a very different backcast from the one delivering the fly forward. Perhaps the most common example is where a side backcast is needed, but a vertical forward cast is required. Such is the case when making a stack cast, casting shooting heads, casting weighted flies, and some other casts in this book. Even when dry-fly fishing, you may want to combine the power and efficiency of a sidearm-style stroke with the accuracy of a vertical cast that comes straight over the rod tip.

Sidearm Backcast, Vertical Forward Cast

Begin the cast with the rod low. You can make a vertical or side cast. Here we are making a side cast.

As soon as the line end leaves the surface, make the backcast.

Bring the rod around for a side cast.

Allow the line to almost straighten.

Make the forward cast.

Speed up and stop the rod to form a nice loop.

Allow the loop to unroll away from the rod tip. When the loop is well away from the tip, you can start to lower the rod.

Continue lowering the rod.

CHAPTER 5

Hauling

The single and double haul are two of the most important techniques you can master. The single haul is nothing more than a pull with the line hand while the rod hand is making the cast. When you make two single hauls, one corresponding to the front cast and the other to the backcast, you are double hauling. Double hauls help you load the rod and generate higher line speeds and are useful for everything from delivering a dry fly a short distance to propelling a huge streamer to a billfish.

There are two parts to any casting stroke: an acceleration (short or long) of the rod and then a stop. The acceleration of the rod accomplishes two things: It causes the line to increase its speed either away from or toward the target and bends the rod, storing energy. Following this motion is the speed-up-and-stop that causes the line to unroll to the target. Most anglers use the haul for the first part of a cast, the acceleration. By hauling the line, it goes faster and deepens the bend in the rod, storing additional energy, which results in a longer cast. But to improve the efficiency of the haul, the line hand should mirror the rod hand during a cast. To understand how to improve the double haul, try this experiment: Make several false casts using the double haul, and on the final forward cast, accelerate the rod and release the line after the acceleration but *without* making the speed-up-and-stop! Hauling increased the line speed and deepened the bend in the rod, but when you released the line, it traveled only a short distance. Repeat the experiment, but this time add a speed-up-and-stop to the forward cast, and the line sizzles toward the target. Without a stop, most of the energy is wasted.

Use the haul like a gear shift to change line speed. When you want to cast farther, haul faster; don't try to overpower your rod hand.

The length of a double haul is dictated by fishing conditions and what you want to accomplish. When casting a dry fly, the haul may only be a few inches. To throw a heavy line and weighted fly into a stiff breeze, the haul may be extra long. One of the keys to efficient hauling is to pull on the line during the rod's acceleration. If the rod is accelerated a short distance, so is the haul. If a longer acceleration occurs, the haul mirrors the length of the acceleration. To improve hauling efficiency, the moment the haul is completed on the backcast, raise your line hand toward the rod butt to reduce any slack. Body movement helps when making longer casts or when extra effort is required while hauling. If you stand squarely facing the target, you can only move the rod back so far. But if you drop your right foot back to the rear (if you are a right-handed caster) and swivel your upper body so your chest is at right angles to the target (you can still look at the target), you can bring your casting arm and rod farther to the rear. Remember Principle 4: The longer the rod moves through the stroke, the more it aids the effort, and the longer the rod is swept forward, the longer the haul can be. This further increases line speed and loads the rod.

When you need more out of a cast, never get it with the rod hand; instead, change the hauling speed. Most people haul at the same speed for every cast, but a single or double haul is like a gearshift, and the speed of the haul should change for fishing conditions. Try this experiment to improve your double haul. Make a series of false casts but with every other cast, move your line hand faster. You will immediately note that as the line hand increases speed on the haul, the line travels faster. To learn how to haul faster without casting too hard with the rod hand (a common tendency), try holding the rod with only your thumb and first two fingers (with ladies who may not be as strong as men, I recommend holding the rod with the thumb and three fingers). It is impossible to overpower the rod holding it this way, and you will quickly learn to increase hauling speed without overpowering the rod hand.

During the haul, the action of your line hand should mirror your speed-up-and-stop casting stroke to gain more line speed and distance. The shorter and faster the rod tip moves during that speed-up-and-stop, the farther the line will unroll. To make the most effective double haul, you must mirror the motion of the rod. Most fishermen haul on the line continuously throughout the backcast and again throughout the forward cast, which is applying the same effect to the cast as if the rod sweeps backward and forward like a windshield wiper, without employing the speed-up-and-stop of the rod tip. Like the rod stroke, the most efficient haul should have two parts: a relatively long pulling on the line (to mirror the cast's first part) and a short, fast speed-up-and-stop (to mirror the cast's second part). When the rod speeds up and stops, the hauling hand should greatly accelerate in a short, fast speed-up-and-stop motion that mirrors the rod tip's action. The rod tip's speed-up-and-stop and the haul's short, fast speed-up-and-stop should be simultaneous. The long pull on the line (a windshield-wiper stroke) helps bend or load the rod. If the speed-up-and-stop of the tip and the greatly accelerated second phase of the haul start and stop at the same time, line speed will dramatically increase and you'll shoot more line.

I present the photo sequences here first on the grass and then in the air, as I like to teach my students. Casting on the grass seems to work well for most people because it allows them to slow everything down, watch what they are doing, and correct their own mistakes.

HAULING ON GRASS

Learning to double haul is difficult because there is so much to do in such a short time. I teach my students to haul on the grass first because at the end of each cast they can examine and evaluate the forward and backcasts individually. With this method, I have taught many people how to double haul in a few minutes. Of course, they will have to practice to perfect it. The slower someone performs the early motions, the faster they learn them. The faster you try to learn the technique, the longer it takes to learn. Do this exceptionally slowly and allow the line to fall to the grass after each back and forward cast. Then do not make another cast until you've determined how poorly or well you made that particular cast. After you have made a number of good lawn double hauls, try making longer pulls on the line during each back and forward cast. When things are going well, begin false casting while double hauling. If the false casting goes badly, return to the lawn and practice with slow motions. Within one or two practice sessions, you'll learn the double haul.

The line hand should return close to the reel after each haul. If you spread the two hands apart as the rod makes another cast, the hands move toward each other, creating slack that must be removed before casting can begin. Returning the line hand each time close to the reel before starting the next cast eliminates slack, which not only makes your cast inefficient but can also result in the line tangling in the reel.

Hauling on Grass

Start with about 20 feet of fly line plus the leader outside the rod tip. The cast will be made sideways and close to the grass. Do not throw an elevated cast.

Your line hand is close to the reel. Your elbow will stay on the imaginary shelf, and your thumb begins the cast behind the reel handle. Your wrist should not twist throughout the cast.

Slowly slide the rod tip back just above the grass. Your line hand follows the reel.

Make a speed-up-and-stop to throw the backcast inches above the grass. At the same time you are accelerating on the backcast, pull quickly only a few inches with your line hand. This is a single haul.

As the backcast unrolls behind, rotate your body and position the rod opposite the target well behind you. Later you will learn to make longer hauls on the line, but for a beginner, the short haul makes for faster learning. It is important to turn your body. Later when you want to cast longer by turning your body, the rod is able to travel farther back, making a longer and more efficient stroke on the forward cast. You are also able to examine what you did right or wrong on the hauling backcast.

Before the backcast ends, move your line hand back in front of the reel. The cast will end. Allow the line to lie on the grass and examine how well you made the cast.

Slowly begin moving your rod hand forward with your line hand moving forward close to the reel. And if you are confused, stop—think about what to do and then continue slowly forward.

Continue to slowly move the rod forward just above the grass. Concentrate on the fact that you are going to make a forward cast and haul at the same time. A caution—almost everyone has more trouble perfecting the forward haul than the back one—so don't be discouraged if at first things go poorly. The slower you do the exercise, the more time you have to consider and practice what to do correctly.

Simultaneously accelerate the rod and pull on the line (hauling) a short distance to make the forward cast.

As you finish the cast, allow the line to fall to the ground and make sure your line hand has returned to its position in front of the reel. Again think about what you have done right and wrong. Once you have the technique going well, make the back and forward casts faster—and then elevate the rod and try hauling with a side cast so you can watch the line. Eventually you'll make a mistake. Place the line on the grass and repeat the early practice session. Usually in several such practice sessions, you will be hauling well.

Hauling on the Water

If you have trouble stopping the haul at the same time that you speed up and stop with your rod hand, let the line fall to the water, slow things down, and start over. This is a relatively long cast, and the haul is long. For a shorter cast, you would only need a short haul. When practicing this on the water, the water helps deepen the load in the rod.

Lower the rod tip to the surface and remove any slack.

Your line hand should follow the rod as it is lifted. Watch the end of the line.

Lift the rod to move the line toward you and off the water.

The moment the line end leaves the water, the rod and line hand should begin accelerating.

If you need a longer cast or more speed, the rod and line hand accelerate simultaneously over a longer stroke.

Do not leave your hauling hand well away from the rod. This creates slack as the rod hand moves forward that must be removed before the forward cast begins. It also may cause the line to tangle around the rod butt or reel.

It is vital that your rod hand's speed-up-and-stop and the hauling stop at the same time. It is the abruptness of the stop that is so important in projecting the line away from or toward the target. A common mistake is to continue to haul after the backcast speed-up-and-stop, which causes the rod to continue to flex, wasting energy.

The moment the hauling motion stops, move your hand toward the rod butt.

Just before the backcast unrolls, your line hand should be positioned near the rod butt.

Continue to accelerate both hands.

Just before the line unrolls, the rod and line hand begin accelerating forward.

Both hands simultaneously stop at the end of the forward cast.

If you want to control the cast, shoot the line through your hand.

Just before the fly touches down, the rod line moves near the rod.

When the line has almost completely unrolled toward the target, lower the rod while still controlling the shooting line.

All line has been shot through the guides, and you can place the line in your rod hand to begin a retrieve.

HAULING SIDEARM (LONG CAST)

The longer the line is outside the rod tip before making the last cast, the greater the potential distance. Of course, at some point you can overload the rod with too much line, but most casters don't load the rod well enough. One way to extend line is by a series of false casts. However, if each false cast is not just right, the final cast suffers.

A better way is to first extend a long line on the water in front of you. If the rod tip starts low, it pulls against the line held by surface tension. The longer the stroke, the more the rod loads, attempting to free the line from the water. A much deeper bend develops by pulling against the water's tension than by false casting in the air. Couple the rod stroke with the double haul to make extra-long casts.

It is less efficient if the rod is raised vertically for a long backcast (either false casting or lifting line from the water). During a vertical stroke, the rod loads mostly in the tip, the weakest portion of the rod. Line can only be lifted from the water until the rod is vertical. With some line remaining on the water and forced to make the cast, many fly fishermen then overpower the stroke, causing the tip to dip downward on the stop, producing a sag in the cast. To make a backcast without sag, the rod tip must stop while it is rising.

A much more efficient method of making an extra long cast is to position as much line on the water as the angler can lift for the backcast. The lower the tip at the beginning, the more line you can lift and the more likely you will make the speed-up-and-stop while the tip is rising. With a side cast, the rod can continue to lift line until the rod tip is beyond your body. This loads the rod deeper, which aids the longer cast. Start the side cast with the tip near the surface, so the rod is still rising when the line end exits the water, enabling a backcast with a flat, tight loop directing all energy away from the target.

> *A good backcast begins with the rod tip low to the water and ends with the tip rising.*

Hauling Sidearm (Long Cast)

When picking up a long line, make sure the rod is low and the tip near the surface. The higher the rod at the beginning of the cast, the shorter the backcast stroke, and it is more difficult to stop the tip from rising.

Your thumb is behind the rod handle away from the target; your elbow is on the imaginary shelf as the line lifts from the water.

Your elbow tracks along the shelf, and your thumb stays behind the handle away from the target. Your body pivots, shifting weight to the rear and assisting with the lift. Make a haul during the time the rod is accelerating back. Note that the rod has loaded until it bends almost to the handle—much deeper than with a normal vertical backcast.

Swivel your upper body, aiding the cast as the rod and hauling hand continue to accelerate. The moment the line exits the water, make the speed-up-and-stop. To make the stop more positive, stop hauling. If you continue to haul, as many anglers do, some of the stop's effect is lost. Speed up and stop when the line end comes out of the water.

Because the rod tip stopped while rising, a flat line and tight loop backcast delivers all the line directly away from the target. To get an even longer stroke for the forward cast, extend your rod hand more to the rear and shift your body back farther. Because the rod tip stopped while rising, the energy is delivered directly away from the target, and no line sag develops. Because the arm was extended after the speed-up-and-stop, your elbow was raised slightly from the shelf but did not affect the cast.

As soon as the speed-up-and-stop and haul end, raise your rod line hand toward the rod butt as the line unrolls back.

Just before the line unrolls, your arm is fully extended by the backward drift. The line is still moving toward the rod butt and most of your body's weight has shifted well to the rear. Your chest is now 90 degrees from the target, allowing you to extend the rod nearly parallel to the surface, making a longer forward stroke possible. Most double haulers turn the upper body only about 45 degrees, losing much of the possible forward stroke.

Your line hand has moved up to just in front of the reel. A common fault with double hauling is that the line hand is positioned well forward of the rod butt. As your rod hand moves forward, it produces slack between the two hands that must be removed before the forward cast begins. If your line hand is just in front of the rod butt, no slack occurs, and the moment the rod begins the forward cast, the line end is moving. It also eliminates troublesome line wrapping around the rod butt or reel during the forward cast.

Just before the line unrolls, begin the forward cast. Your line hand is just in front of the rod butt.

Your thumb is behind the handle away from the target. Your elbow slides forward, staying on the imaginary shelf, and your body pivots, aiding the cast. The acceleration of the rod and the haul are simultaneous.

Your body has pivoted back to the start of the cast. Your thumb is behind the rod handle away from the target, and your elbow slides forward on the shelf. This allows the rod tip to speed up and stop straight ahead, producing a flat line and tight loop. The haul ceased as the rod tip stopped.

If you need maximum distance, release the line. If you need an accurate cast, allow the line to flow through your hand until the fly stops over the target. I find it helps with a slightly climbing forward cast if you lift your elbow slightly and fully extend your arm when line is shot over a long distance.

If you lower the rod immediately after the speed-up-and-stop, the loop opens and energy is lost. Allow the line loop to unroll well away from the rod tip before lowering the rod tip as the fly nears the target.

The line continues shooting forward.

As the cast ends, lower the rod to a fishing position.

COMMON HAULING MISTAKES

One of the most common problems that I see with hauling is continuing to pull on the line after your rod hand stops. The more abruptly the rod stops, the more energy is directed at the target. The rod and line hand should mirror one another and work in unison. When both hands stop at the same time, all energy is directed at the target.

> ***The haul should mirror the speed-up-and-stop of the rod hand.***

To see this in action, try this: Make a fairly long backcast, and allow the line to lie straight on the ground behind you.

Make a forward cast and continue pulling on the line after the rod hand speeds up and stops, and then release the line. Repeat this several times. Then make the same cast several times with the line lying on the ground behind you. Now make sure that both hands stop at the same time. Your loop will be tighter, and you'll cast farther.

Incorrect: Hauling after the Rod Hand Stops

The cast begins with the rod low and all slack removed from the line.

As soon as the line leaves the water, I accelerate the rod and my line hand to make the backcast.

I lift the rod to remove the line from the water; my line hand follows the rod.

As the backcast ends I stop accelerating both hands.

As the backcast is unrolling, my line hand approaches the rod butt.

The speed-up-and-stop occurs, but my line hand continues hauling, and the rod tip doesn't stop.

The forward cast begins with both hands accelerating simultaneously.

Even as the rod is lowering, I am still hauling on the line, detracting from the forward cast.

CATCHING LINE

Another common problem when hauling is to pull downward on the line during the backcast and leave your line hand well away from the rod. As the rod is swept forward, whether your line hand is stationary or brought upward, slack is increased between your line hand and your rod hand. You must remove this slack before the rod can pull on the line. To illustrate this, make a backcast and allow the line to fall to the ground behind you with the line hand well away from the rod. With the rod pointed at the line end, slowly move the rod forward toward your line hand and note that until your rod hand is close to your line hand, the line end remains stationary on the grass. Leaving your line hand well away from the rod before the forward cast is why so many times after the cast is completed, the line tangles around the rod butt or reel.

Incorrect: Catching Line

The rod begins low, and all slack has been removed. I lift the rod to remove the line from the water.

The line hand makes a long pull.

As soon as the line end leaves the water, I accelerate both my hands.

Because of the long hauling motion and leaving the hand so low, the line tends to fall beneath the rod butt as the backcast nears an end.

If my line hand remains in this position on the forward cast, the butt of the rod or the reel will trap the line underneath it.

As I lower the rod, the line will be tangled in either the reel or the rod butt.

As my rod hand moves forward, the line remains trapped under the butt.

No retrieve is possible until the line can be untangled. This could be avoided if I had moved my line hand close to the rod butt as soon as the hauling motion had ceased.

CHAPTER 6

Roll Cast

The basic roll cast is one of the most useful casts that you need to be able to make, whether in salt or fresh water. I use the roll cast for all sorts of things—making casts when there is little or no backcast room behind me, casting sinking lines to the surface of the water before beginning my backcast, picking up a dry fly (roll-cast pickup), and freeing snags from stumps and downed trees. Unfortunately, it is the one cast most often performed poorly, largely because most casting instructors teach it the wrong way.

Only modify the backcast on a roll cast—your forward cast should speed up and stop, going straight ahead or slightly up.

In a good roll cast, you only modify the backcast. You should make the forward cast like you would any other cast, accelerating to a stop and aiming at or slightly above eye level and with as small a loop as possible, unless you need a big loop. Roll casts rely on the stick of the line on the water to load your rod, but too much detracts from your cast.

Here are some important points to consider when making a roll cast:

1. The line being cast must drape outside the tip. If the line is positioned between the angler and the rod on the forward stroke, a tangle occurs.
2. The loop hanging behind the rod prior to the cast (which is called the D loop) must be aligned opposite the direction of the forward cast. If not, energy is wasted to correctly align it during the forward cast, and tangles often occur. The longer the required cast, the larger the D loop should be behind the caster.
3. You must bring sinking lines to the surface before making the roll cast.

4. The amount of line lying on the surface in front of you is critical. Surface tension grips a floating fly line on the water. What is needed for a decent roll cast is for enough of the line to be held by surface tension so that it offers enough resistance against the rod sweeping forward to properly bend and load it. If too much line lies on the water, most of the forward cast energy is wasted pulling the line free of the surface tension, and a poor cast results. When making roll casts that are longer than about 25 feet, there is no need for the line to pause and be gripped by the surface tension. The weight of the line outside the tip is enough to load the rod, similar to Spey casting.

You get the best results when making the forward roll cast with a floating line if no more than a rod length of line lies on the surface in front of you. I have met few fly fishermen who are aware that having the proper amount of line on the water is critical to good roll-casting technique.

5. Begin a backcast by raising the rod tip to draw the floating line back. A brief stop is mandatory (only the space of a heartbeat or two is necessary). Surface tension grips the line the moment the line stops. This gives the rod something to pull against, allowing it to make a forward roll cast. If the floating line is drawn back and there is no stop to let surface grip the line, the line will continue to speed back before going forward, wasting energy, and generally a poor cast results.

Once a sinking line is positioned on the surface, you must immediately begin the forward cast. A delay allows the line to sink, making it difficult to cast. There is enough tension to properly load the rod if the forward roll cast starts as soon as the sinking line is positioned on the surface.

With longer roll casts, it is best to place the end of the line within 10 feet or even slightly behind you and allow it to barely kiss the water. Do not pause with longer line. The D loop will begin to fall, creating slack that has to be removed before a forward cast can begin. Once the line end touches the water, make a forward cast. The moving weight of the line will easily load the rod.

Because we want to get off on the right foot, I'll show the way that I recommend making a basic roll cast (side and rear views) and then show a photo sequence of how many people learn to make roll casts, which is the way that I first learned, and incorrect. After that, we'll go over a more efficient variation of this basic roll cast.

BASIC ROLL CAST

Most fly fishermen perform this useful cast poorly, primarily because of a poor forward cast. They tend to aim the rod tip downward, rather than straight ahead, and make a large sweeping motion rather than a short speed-up-and-stop. Videos and books for years have taught us to make a roll cast by driving the rod over and downward, which means the line will roll over and downward and collapse in a pile in front of us. But even though we need to modify the backcast, we should make a normal forward cast to ensure that the fly travels above the water and not down in front of us. There are reasons for changing the angle of the forward cast in a roll cast, such as for the ridding grass cast (see page 273), but you should generally focus on coming through in a straight line.

Basic Roll Cast

Begin the cast with the rod tip near or at the surface.

Slowly raise the rod tilted slightly away from your body. If you bring the rod back and do not tilt it, the forward cast often entangles in the line or rod.

Continue to slowly raise the rod. Lifting it too quickly will often create surface disturbance, alerting fish nearby. Lifting the rod draws the line end toward you.

Continue bringing the rod tip up and back. For a short cast, imagine you are sliding the line back on the surface.

Tip the rod tip back when the line end is no more than 10 feet from you.

With a short cast, you must pause with the rod long enough so the line end stops moving. It can only be a heartbeat, but this lets surface tension grip the line so the rod has something to pull against. With an extended line, there is no need to stop since the weight of the line will load the rod—such as with the switch cast or long-distance roll cast.

With a short cast, as soon as the line end stops moving, surface tension grips the line. This allows the rod to pull against surface tension to load the rod for the cast. If the line end is not allowed to stop, it is very difficult to make a cast.

During the entire forward cast, keep your elbow on the shelf, and your rod hand should accelerate at the same height. This will direct all of the energy of the cast straight ahead. If you hold the rod vertically, the line may crash into the rod or part of the line, resulting in a tangle. With any roll cast, the line should drape away from the rod and angler to eliminate the tangle.

Continue to accelerate the rod hand forward, and wait until the last possible moment before making the speed-up-and-stop. This results in a normal forward cast with a tight loop. The shorter the speed-up-and-stop at the end of the stroke, the tighter will be the loop. A helpful hint in producing a nice tight loop on the forward cast is not to make the final speed-up-and-stop until your rod hand is in front of your body. If you speed up and stop while your hand is even with or behind your body, a long speed-up-and-stop occurs and results in a larger loop.

Do not immediately lower the rod after the speed-up-and-stop. Instead, allow the loop to continue unrolling toward the target.

When the line loop is well away from the rod tip, lower it.

Continue to lower the rod tip to the fishing position before the fly touches the water.

Rear View of the Roll Cast

Here is a rear view of a basic roll cast. Note how the rod is angled to the side. In all roll casts, you should angle the rod tip slightly away from the body so the line drapes outward. If you bring the rod tip back vertically or tilt it inward on the forward cast, the line will tangle around the rod.

Begin with the rod tip close to the water.

Draw the line and rod directly away from the target area with the rod tip tilted at an angle.

Continue drawing back the rod.

And keep bringing it back, forming a belly in the line. Note that your elbow remains on the imaginary shelf and your rod hand is kept low.

Keep bringing the rod tip back until it is just past your head, forming a nice D loop in the line, and stop the rod so that the fly line end stops. Pause for a heartbeat. With every roll cast, the D loop in the line should be positioned opposite the forward cast target.

The line has formed a good D loop. After a brief pause, start accelerating forward toward the target.

Continue accelerating the rod forward with your elbow on the shelf and your rod hand traveling straight ahead.

If you delay the speed-up-and-stop at the end of the cast until the last moment and your rod tip stops going straight ahead, the tight loop aims all the cast's energy at the target.

Wait for the line to unroll.

Start to drop your rod tip.

Continue dropping the tip, timing it with the line unrolling.

Near the end of the cast, lower the rod to a fishing position.

INEFFICIENT ROLL CAST

The roll cast that I first learned—and the one that I see many anglers making today—does the opposite of all these things. It goes like this: Gently draw back the floating fly line until it forms a D slightly behind. Raise your elbow and bend your wrist. Stop the rod just past vertical (sometimes you need to start this way because of obstructions behind you), and raise your elbow as you come forward, often driving the rod tip toward the surface with your wrist. Not only does this motion not allow your rod to help you very much, but you throw the line around the biggest possible circle that you can, wasting energy and piling the line. The line goes in the direction the rod tip stops, and if you look at many of the books and videos, you will notice that the tip of the rod is driving toward the water directly in front of it, which is why the line most frequently piles up when this kind of cast is made. I think of all the casts most frequently made by the average fly fisherman, the roll cast is the one performed most poorly.

Inefficient Roll Cast

This is the typical inefficient position to begin a forward roll cast. My elbow is elevated off the shelf, and my wrist is bent.

I start the forward roll cast by flexing my wrist forward while dropping my hand and elbow and making a long sweeping motion of the rod, which develops a large, rounded line loop.

The rod stops in a downward motion, creating a large inefficient loop.

This results in wasted energy that doesn't go toward the target. Stopping the rod tip in a downward motion causes the front of the line and leader to be aimed at the surface short of the target area.

Note that a portion of the front of the line lies in a crumpled heap on the water and the leader is vertically falling.

All of this slack line and piled leader is typical of many roll casts.

Inefficient Roll Cast

Here is a close-up sequence of the hand motions. Note how my elbow is off the shelf and my wrist is bent.

My elbow is far off the shelf as I elevate my rod hand.

I bend my wrist, bringing the tip of the rod even farther back, and also continue to raise my elbow. This roll cast is doomed.

I begin the speed-up-and-stop well above my head. I drive my arm forward, but instead of stopping, I go straight ahead. (Remember that a forward roll cast is like any other forward cast—only the backcast is modified.)

I continue down, aiming at the water and moving the rod tip through a large arc.

The line puddles up in front of me. By making a continuous casting stroke beginning in a vertical position and sweeping downward to the water, the rod is forced to throw the line around a wide circle—with little of the line being directed to the target area. The line also goes in the direction the rod tip stops, which directs the line end and leader at the surface in front of me.

A MORE EFFICIENT ROLL CAST

To make the most efficient roll cast, bring the rod and rod hand back as far as you possibly can for the existing fishing conditions so you can use the rod to help you make the cast. If you keep your hand low, your elbow on the shelf, and your thumb behind the cork, and you stop the tip in the direction you want the line to go, you are going to throw a fast, tight loop.

When making a roll cast, you may have to modify the backcast, but you should always try to make a normal forward cast with a tight loop directed straight ahead, not aimed at the water or the desired target. To make the most efficient cast, bring the rod back well behind you if fishing conditions permit. The longer you take the rod to the rear, the more it will aid in making the cast—the fourth casting principle. Extending your rod tip way back is good for some situations where you have overhanging canopy that would prevent bringing your rod straight up and back in a conventional roll cast. With this cast, you can extend your rod tip back and relatively low to avoid hitting your rod tip on tree limbs and other streamside obstructions. After a brief pause to allow surface tension to grip the line and help load the rod, bring your rod hand forward, staying at the same height throughout the forward cast. If the tip stops in a downward direction, some of the line will be thrown downward. If the rod tips stops in the direction of the target, the line will go in that direction.

To get a nice tight loop, accelerate your rod hand forward but do not make the short speed-up-and-stop until your rod hand is in front of your body. Beginning the speed-up-and-stop before this results in a wide wasted loop. If your elbow rises off the shelf, then the loop will enlarge, wasting energy. Keeping your rod hand and elbow moving directly toward the target will ensure all the energy goes toward the target—as would any good forward cast. Most people who use this technique and still have some trouble start the speed-up-and-stop when their hand is either slightly behind or even with their bodies, and that means they are going to make a longer speed-up-and-stop, and so the tip of the rod, which is not traveling straight, even though the hand is because it is pivoting, is going to throw a bigger loop in the line than we want.

Improved Roll Cast

Begin with the rod tip close to the surface.

Lift the rod slowly with the rod tip angled to the side. Keep your elbow on the imaginary shelf and your rod hand well below your shoulder.

Continue to bring the rod back, drawing the line end closer. Make sure your elbow stays on the shelf and your rod hand is well below your shoulder.

Do not stop the rod, but continue to move it back.

Continue to move the rod well behind you as far as the fishing conditions allow. Your line hand should follow the rod as it is being lifted. If your line hand remained motionless during the lifting, there would be a space between the two hands, and on the forward cast slack would result at first, spoiling the cast.

Extend your rod arm as far back as it can for existing fishing conditions.

For an ideal forward roll cast, the rod should be positioned well back, your elbow on the shelf, and your rod hand low. With roll casts less than 25 feet, the line end resting on the surface should only be a foot in front of you or better, as shown here. This is just enough line on the water to load the rod, but there is no extra line that must be torn free of the water before making the cast.

Don't delay beginning the forward cast, as the D loop will develop slack. Keep your elbow on the shelf, maintaining your rod hand at the same height throughout the forward cast. If your hand travels up and down, the line will do the same. If your hand drops on the forward cast, it will cause the line end and leader to pile. By keeping your rod hand at the same level throughout the forward stroke, you direct all of the energy of the cast toward the target. Accelerate the rod forward, loading it. The longer the desired cast, the longer the forward acceleration.

Remember that the shorter the speed-up-and-stop, the tighter the loop. After accelerating, bring the rod to a brief, quick speed-up-and-stop to form a small loop just as in a normal forward cast. The line goes in the direction the rod tip stops. If the rod tip stops downward, the line will go in that direction and can end up in a pile on the surface. Stop the rod tip in the direction you would for a normal forward cast to get a loop like this.

If the forward roll cast is made properly, the line loop should never appear to be round, which means much of the energy has been diverted around a circle. Instead, it should resemble a good forward cast with a tight loop, and the line from the rod tip to the unrolling loop should be parallel with the water and not have a deep sag.

As the fly nears the target, lower the rod tip to the fishing position.

SHORT SWITCH CAST

The switch cast is a variation of a basic Spey cast that doesn't involve a change of direction. Because it allows you to easily place a lot of line behind you, it is the easiest way to make exceptionally long roll casts, especially if you include a single haul on the forward cast. But I often make shorter switch casts, when I want to easily cast 20 to 30 feet, because I sometimes prefer the fluid motion of a backcast and well-placed anchor (the place where the fly line lands on the water) over slowly dragging the rod back, as for a conventional roll cast. You achieve, more or less, the same result as short distances, but practicing the short switch first will limber you up for the longer ones required for longer distances (see page 400).

In these photos I am coming back vertically, but you can come back at any angle for the backcast, and following the principles, the longer you want to make a cast, the farther back you should extend the arm. Compare this cast with the longer one in the chapter on distance casting.

Short Switch Cast

Begin with the rod tip near the surface.

Draw the line end toward you by slowly raising the rod as it tilts slightly away from you. If the rod is raised too quickly, the surface disturbance may spook nearby fish.

When the rod reaches a vertical position, you can no longer drag the line toward you. But the line end is still too far away. Tilt the rod outward and accelerate the tip in a short circular motion. Do not make this motion too fast, or the line will travel too far behind you.

The perfect position is when the line end falls to the surface no more than a few feet in front to just behind you. This is just enough surface tension to load the rod on the forward cast. Only practice will teach you to position the line end properly.

Wait until the line end stops moving and immediately accelerate forward. If you wait too long, the D loop will begin to fall, creating slack that must be removed with rod motion before a forward cast can be made.

During the forward cast, your elbow stays on the shelf and your rod hand moves in a straight line toward the target area. Delay the speed-up-and-stop until the final moment of the cast to create a small loop. Stop the rod going toward the target, and do not follow through.

Allow the line loop to unroll well away from the rod tip before starting to lower the rod tip.

Just before the line unrolls, lower the rod to a fishing position.

Part III

FISHING CASTS

CHAPTER 7

Drag-Free Drifts

I once knew one of the sorriest casters in the world. He would sweep the rod tip to the water, and his loops were 12 feet wide. But he would catch lots of fish. As he swept the rod tip down toward the water, the line and leader would stack up, and he could get incredible long drifts with his fly before drag set in. His poor casting technique turned out to be excellent fishing form. Better casters, who know how to stop the rod and let the line unroll, tend to pull out all the slack. I am not telling you this to discourage you from becoming a better caster but to encourage you to learn how to make both controlled tight loop casts and controlled slack line casts. You may be able to catch a lot of fish with poor casting skills, but I guarantee you'll be able to catch a lot more if you improve your casting.

George Harvey showed me and thousands of other anglers that you need to have slack in front of the fly to make good drag-free drifts. He taught tens of thousands of students during (and after) his tenure at Penn State and in his demos and presentations. Harvey developed an elaborate leader formula to help even beginners get the slack that they needed, but I have discovered over the years that if you know the fundamentals of casting, you can put the necessary curves in your line and leader without that formula. Though leader designs can be important, the most important factor is not the leader, but the one who casts it.

Trout then weren't as wise or sophisticated as they are today. George's lesson now is even more important. To present the fly so that it drifts naturally to the fish, you must have a wave or curve in the leader immediately in front of the fly and the fly line must be upstream of the fly. If the leader remains

You must make the forward cast on the reach (and stack) cast as gently as possible. Because you need to place line upstream, if the line travels too fast on the forward cast, you won't have enough time to lay the line over.

straight inches in front of the fly, moving currents will act on it. Pick up a garden hose lying on the grass with slack in the hose immediately in front of the sprinkler. Start walking with the hose, and the moment the hose straightens in front of the sprinkler, you begin to drag it. The main thing in dry-fly fishing is having slack in the leader. You won't get drag as long as there is slack in front of the fly. Your leader doesn't need to land in perfect S curves. On some technical streams, anglers use 17-foot leaders and long tippets that fall in messes, but all that slack allows the flies to float perfectly. Fish come up through the mess of tippet to take the fly. Setting the hook with all that slack is not as difficult as it seems.

There are two types of basic leader designs. Bass or saltwater leaders are designed to straighten so that you can manipulate the fly after casting it. Good trout leaders are designed to collapse. Most of the time when you are dry-fly or nymph fishing for trout, you want to be able to make a cast that allows the current to bring the fly to the fish naturally and drag-free, and you do not want a leader that turns over straight. The front end should have some waves in it.

REACH CAST

Trout expect food to be delivered in a natural manner and will almost always refuse a dry fly that drags across the surface, unless it happens to be imitating a natural that is also skittering. The single most important factor for successful dry-fly fishing is the ability to make a cast that presents the fly drag-free and naturally to the trout. When fishing across the current, anytime the fly line drifts downstream from the fly, the

162

belly in the line will begin dragging the fly. The reach cast presents all of the fly line and leader upstream of the dry fly, allowing for a longer drag-free drift.

While the reach cast is considered a freshwater casting technique, it can pay off in the salt. One example comes to mind: The falling tide in Waltz Key Channel was carrying with it a small crab hatch. These little crabs couldn't fight the swift tide so they drifted along in it, and a few permit were sipping down these morsels near the surface. Eventually I figured out that the permit wouldn't take the fly unless it was drifting drag-free, and the reach cast was the perfect way to do that.

The reach cast is one cast where high line speed is not usually desirable. You must make the forward cast on the reach (and stack) cast as gently as possible. Because you need

to place line upstream, if the line is traveling too fast on the forward cast, you won't have enough time to lay the line over. If you aim the line too low on the forward cast, you won't have enough time to place the line upstream. Also, it is important to feed line as you reach upstream so that you don't pull slack out of the line when you reach.

The stack cast develops controlled waves in the front of the fly line and leader. If you combine the stack and the reach cast, you position the line upstream of a fly with multiple waves in the leader and forward line to deliver an incredibly long drag-free cast.

Because the reach cast is so important—and I find that so many anglers perform it incorrectly—I am going to show top, front, and close-up views of the critical steps for making a good reach cast.

Reach Cast

Begin the cast with some slack line in your hand. Make a soft, elevated forward cast toward the target.

The high, slow cast gives you time to lay the fly line upstream by tilting the rod over instantly after the speed-up-and-stop.

Feed slack into the cast as you continue to reach upstream. Allow the slack to flow through your cupped first finger and thumb so you have constant control of the line.

Slack continues to feed into the cast as the rod nears a parallel position. This is an important part of an effective reach cast.

As the cast ends, the line is well upstream of the fly. The elevated cast helps stack waves in the leader as the fly falls to the surface, ensuring a drag-free drift. That slack that you fed has not affected the forward portion of the cast.

All slack has been fed through your hand as the cast ends.

Reach Cast (Front View, Correct)

There are reasons why you do not want to drop the line from your hand when making a reach cast. Occasionally a cast is made that is traveling wrong. If the line is shooting through your hand toward the target, you realize it's going wrong. If you control the line, you can make another backcast and reposition the forward cast. You can also trap the line when the fly has reached the target, ensuring accuracy. If the slack line is allowed to flow freely through the guides at the end of the cast, the angler has to look down to recapture the line, and that could be when the fish strikes.

Front View of the Reach Cast

Begin the forward cast just before the line unrolls on the backcast.

Make the cast slow and high to give you time to lay the line upstream. Many, when learning the reach cast, throw the cast too fast and low. Before they can lay the line upstream, it is already in the water.

The moment the rod tip speeds up and stops, the rod starts to lay over. The farther the rod is placed upstream, the more line is positioned on the water upstream of the fly.

The rod follows the line as it begins falling. Lean your body and extend your arm to allow line to shoot through your hand so as not to affect the forward portion of the cast. Feed slack through your line hand as you lay the rod over to ensure a delicate cast with the right amount of slack. If you hold the line, you can pull the slack from the front end and spoil the cast.

Continue to allow slack line to flow through your hand. Allowing line to flow through your hand gives you control throughout the reach cast. The farther you place the line upstream, the longer the drag-free drift. Lower the rod tip as the line unrolls.

Close-up of the Reach Cast

Begin the cast with the rod low and all slack removed from the line.

Raise the rod to lift the line free of the surface.

As soon as the line end leaves the surface, make the backcast.

Just before the line unrolls, begin the forward cast.

Make a slow, high cast so you have time to lay the rod and line over.

The moment you speed up and stop, lay the rod over upstream.

As you lay the rod upstream, shoot slack line through your hand.

Allow the line to continue flowing through your hand as the rod positions the line upstream of the fly.

By permitting the slack line to flow through your hand, you have complete control of the cast.

The line and leader have landed upstream of the fly.

Incorrect: Holding the Line During the Reach Cast

To make a good reach, you need to place some slack line upstream of the fly. Not only must you place the line upstream of the leader and fly, but you must make an accurate cast. If you hold onto the line as you reach upstream, then the slack, instead of feeding from the line hand, must come from the far end of the line, which jerks the line, leader, and fly back and spoils your accuracy. This is a common fault with fly casters using the reach cast. This sequence illustrates why you should not hold onto the line while laying the rod upstream.

I make a slow, elevated cast toward the target.

The loop unrolls. As I lay the rod over upstream, I am tightly holding the line.

I position the rod upstream to place slack in the line.

By holding the line in hand, I pull the slack from the front of the line instead of feeding it from my hand.
Because no slack is being fed from my line hand, the rod begins to pull back the line and fly.

Note how the rod is pulling the fly and line back. This results in shortening the line and often straightening the front
of the line and leader, spoiling a good drag-free drift. For a good cast, the slack must originate at the line hand.

Incorrect: Front View of Holding the Line

Note how I hold onto the fly line, even pulling it back a little bit, removing all the slack from this reach cast.

Just before the backcast unrolls, I begin a high forward cast.

I lay the rod and line to the side to place slack line on the water.

I am firmly holding the line, not feeding any line through my hand as the rod continues to the side.

I am trapping the line in my hand as I lay the rod over.

The reach cast involves laying slack line upstream. If my hand holds the fly line as the rod sweeps to the side, all slack must come from the end of the line and leader. This can affect accuracy and reduce the length of a drag-free cast.

AERIAL MENDS

You can mend line several different ways. The most common way that anglers mend line is to wait until it is on the water and then pick it up and place it upstream or downstream of the fly to affect the way it drifts or swims in the water. You mend upstream to slow down the currents' drag on your fly, and you mend downstream to amplify the drag and swim your fly faster. When you make an aerial mend, you essentially throw a calculated shock wave in your fly line so that it lands on the water in a curve, and another on-the-water mend is not necessary until the current pulls the first curve out of your line. This cast is ideal for when you have to cast across stream where there are variations in the current flow.

The mend must have enough time during the flight of the cast to be positioned where you want it. With a little practice,

you can position the upstream mend at any distance, from slightly behind the leader to directly in front of you. The farther out you want the mend, the sooner after the stop you move the rod tip. For a mend way out near the end of the line, wiggle the tip immediately after the stop, so that the motions are almost one and the same.

Make the forward cast slowly and with just enough energy, and no more, to get the line out where you want it. Also, aim the cast higher than eye level and make the mend decisively, but don't aggressively wiggle the tip back and forth several times. The front of the leader and line should fall with some soft waves to get a drag-free drift.

Aerial Mends

We are going to make an upstream mend in the current flowing from right to left. Make a slow forward cast at an elevated angle directed toward the target. The high forward cast will give the mend in the line time to flow to the desired position.

In this example, I am making a mend just behind where the leader connects to the fly line. The moment the rod speeds up and stops, flick the rod tip gently to the right, causing a shock wave to the right to flow down the line toward the fly. The flick should be gentle; too much force will spoil the cast. The harder the flick, the greater the size of the shock waves.

The shock is visible as it unrolls toward the target.

As the cast nears completion, lower the rod.

The shock wave has traveled close to the leader as the line begins falling to the surface. The longer the delay of the flick of the rod tip after the speed-up-and-stop, the less distance the shock can travel. With practice, you can position the upstream mend where you choose.

A mend is created upstream and because of the elevated cast, the front of line and leader have fallen in soft waves, ensuring a drag-free float.

If you wait longer before flicking the rod after the speed-up-and-stop, the shock waves can travel only so far. The longer the delay before making the flick, the closer the mend in the line.

SLACK-LEADER CAST

To make a good slack-leader cast, I don't advocate casting with high line speed and stopping the rod sharply to create a shock in order to put slack in the leader. When you shock the rod, it's often hard to tell where the fly is going to go, and you are actually pulling some of the curves out of your line. I prefer to make a controlled soft cast with no shock.

Begin with an elevated forward cast, apply power softly, and after the loop is formed, drop the rod tip to the surface of the water. This gentle cast is accurate and puts lots of slack in

your leader and line. If a high-speed cast is made, the line recoils at the end, jumps back, and ruins the delivery. If you aim the forward cast high enough, this becomes a stack cast. The principles are the same, though you can make this cast without a low backcast. The key is to stop and drop your rod tip gently to the water. The rod must be lowered immediately after the speed-up-and-stop. If not, the line held aloft by the rod tip will sag back, pulling the waves from the line.

Slack-Leader Cast

Begin with an elevated forward cast.

The higher the angle at which you stop, the more waves will develop in the front of the fly line and the leader.

The moment the rod speeds up and stops, begin dropping the rod.

Continue to lower the rod.

As the front of the line begins to fall, the rod tip should be close to the surface.

The front portion of the line and the leader are falling vertically.

This causes the front of the line and the leader to fall in soft, desirable waves.

The fly is falling vertically.

This much slack in the front of the fly line and leader ensures a drag-free drift.

There is a lot of slack in the line, but the fly has landed accurately.

STACK CAST

This cast has been around for a long time and has been called everything from a tower, pile, puddle, and parachute cast. Several casts deliver soft waves in the front of the line and the leader, but I think the most accurate (even at long distances) is the stack cast. When people traditionally make this cast, they start the forward cast with the rod fairly elevated, which makes it difficult to get a high trajectory without tailing the loop. Suppose you stood 15 feet back from a building, and you tried to throw the fly up the side of the building. If you make a conventional backcast, stopping at maybe 2 o'clock or 2:30, you can't do it. If you take the rod low behind you and back, you can throw up along the wall. The low side backcast really helps set you up for a high forward cast. The farther you go back with the rod, the higher you can throw the line.

When making a stack cast, the more slack that you want in the line, the higher you should angle the forward cast, which means the lower to the water that you should make your backcast.

I use this cast most of the time when I want a soft dry-fly presentation. Whenever I have overhead room and there is no stiff breeze, this is my preferred cast for getting lots of drag-free waves in front of the line and leader. I also combine this cast with a reach cast to get an incredibly long drift, which is particularly helpful on larger rivers. The high trajectory and slow speed give you plenty of time to reach way upstream. What too many people do with the reach cast is make it low and fast, and by the time they lay the rod over, the line is already in the water. A stack cast angles the line even higher. The more slack that you want in the line, the higher the elevation of the forward cast so that you give the line and leader time to pile up. If after the speed-up-and-stop the rod remains elevated, the line sagging back from the tip will pull most of the created waves from the leader. The key is to stop and drop.

If you make this cast properly, it is a very gentle cast—you don't shock the rod at all, and it will fall in a perfectly straight line, unless there is a wind, in which case the roll dump (see page 197) is often a better alternative. If you want to make this cast in a wind, you have to try and compensate for the direction that the wind is blowing.

Stack Cast

Start with the rod tip low, and remove all slack from the line.

With this cast, you have more control with a low side backcast. Extend a little more line than what is normally needed to reach the target since the waves placed in the line as it stacks will shorten the cast.

As soon as the line end leaves the water, make the low side backcast.

As the backcast unrolls, the rod is low and well behind you, which makes an elevated forward cast easier.

Begin the forward cast low, and then aim it high.

The cast should be a slow, soft one. If there is too much speed at the end of the cast, the line recoils and spoils the presentation.

At about this point in the stroke, begin the speed-up-and-stop with the rod tip directed upward. Make a gentle speed-up-and-stop, aiming it high, before your hand gets in front of your body. If your hand is well in front of you, a higher cast is more difficult.

Note that the rod has stopped almost in a vertical position, helping to make a towering cast. The higher the cast is aimed, the more waves will stack in the line and leader.

As soon as you make the speed-up-and-stop, immediately lower the rod.

Follow the line with the rod tip as it falls.

If you don't lower the rod immediately, the sag in the line near the rod tip will drag most of the desired waves from the line and leader.

Continue to lower the rod.

Continue to lower the rod.

The front of the line and leader are beginning to fall vertically.

The waves continue to develop in the line and leader as the cast nears the end.

At the end of the cast, much of the forward portion of the line and the leader have fallen to the water with small waves that will get a drag-free drift.

Incorrect: Stack Cast

This demonstrates the wrong way to make a stack cast. It is important to lower the rod immediately after the forward cast speeds up and stops.

I start with the rod low to the water.

I begin the vertical backcast, raising the rod to lift line from the surface.

Instead of making a side backcast, I have stopped the rod in a more vertical position that will make it harder to make an elevated forward cast.

I allow the backcast to nearly straighten.

I direct the forward cast almost parallel to the surface.

The rod sends the line straight ahead. On the speed-up-and-stop, the tight loop has caused the line to travel rapidly forward. The loop is unrolling fast and straight ahead. When my rod hand is this far in front of me, it is more difficult to make a speed-up-and-stop that directs the fly line at an elevated angle.

At the end of the cast, the fast traveling line has bounced against the tip and caused the front end of the line to recoil and turn under.

I keep the rod in an upward position, and the recoiled line begins falling.

Maintaining the rod upright creates a sag that pulls the line back toward the rod and eliminates any waves that might have developed.

Roll Stack Cast

The roll stack cast is helpful when there are obstructions behind you, but you still need a drag-free drift. After you come back for a roll cast, make the forward cast at a high trajectory like a regular stack cast. It is effective from 20 to 60 feet.

Begin with the rod tip close to the water.

Raise the rod to lift line from the water.

Continue to raise the rod.

The moment you lift all the line from the water, make a weak switch cast.

Direct the cast parallel to the surface and not upward.

The intent is to drop most of the line not far behind you. Note that throughout the cast, your rod hand and elbow have stayed on the same plane. You can also just draw the line behind you, forming a D loop as with a regular roll cast.

Ideally, almost all line should be in the air behind you with the fly near your body. Stop the rod low and well back.

Allow the line to touch the surface.

The moment the line falls to the surface, begin a high, towering forward cast. If you delay after the line falls to the water, slack accumulates, affecting the forward cast.

The rod stops just past vertical, directing the fly line in a climbing angle. The intent is to throw the fly line high.

Watch the fly line as it unrolls upward.

The moment you speed up and stop, lower the rod tip. Don't lower it too fast or you will pull back on the falling line.

Continue to lower the rod.

The rod follows the line down until the tip is almost in the water.

Because the line falls almost vertically, the leader and the front of the line fall in small waves.

This cast produces a lot of slack for a drag-free drift of the fly.

ROLL DUMP CAST

I discovered this cast one day on the Gallatin River in Montana. I was fishing along a cut bank where the trout were taking hoppers, and they would dart out, take the fly, and go right back under the bank. If you didn't get your fly into that calm water right next to the bank, you didn't get a fish. I began experimenting with different casts, and I realized that I could make a bad roll cast a good thing by using the pileup of line and leader to my advantage to help me get a longer drag-free float.

The roll dump has since become one of my favorite methods for getting a drag-free drift, especially on smaller streams where there is a slow current near the streambank but the faster water just off the bank causes the fly to drag. Once you make a few roll dump casts, you can get a feel for where to stop the rod and where the line goes so you can begin to make this cast accurately. Once you master this cast, you can make controlled casts within inches of your target. This cast is good up to 35 or 40 feet. This is a modified roll cast where the tip of the rod on the speed-up-and-stop delivers the fly line short of the target. As long as the tip is driving down, it will stack up the front of the line and leader.

How far the fly lands from you is determined by where you direct the rod tip in front of you. If it comes down close to you, then the fly will not go far. If it still comes down toward the water, but at an angle, you can cast farther out. This cast is so effective at piling slack in your leader that sometimes you can throw into a lazy Susan and have the fly go around twice before it starts to drag. If you have any overhanging brush or other obstructions, you can't get in there with a stack cast. The forward cast is too high. With the roll dump, the line travels much closer to the water. Some anglers worry that too much slack will make them miss strikes, but I have never found this to be a problem.

I like to use this cast instead of a stack cast if it is windy. With a stack cast, the wind can blow the line all over the place as the line drifts down. Though the roll dump doesn't work well on quiet water because of the disturbance of the line, it works very well whenever you have any kind of moving water such as riffles.

Roll Dump Cast

Tilt the rod slightly outward and raise it to draw the line end closer.

Raise the rod slowly so as not to make a surface disturbance that may frighten nearby fish.

When the rod is in about this position, make a gentle backcast. This backcast is a variation of the switch cast (see short switch cast, page 157), but you can make this cast by drawing the line back in the regular manner.

When the D loop is behind you and the line close by, begin the forward cast. Make sure you start with the rod in a vertical position.

Accelerate the rod tip around a downward curve to develop a large line loop.

Continue driving the rod tip around a large curve.

Speed up and stop the rod tip in a direction short of where you want the fly to land.

This causes the forward end of the line and the leader to start falling in a vertical manner.

As the forward end of the line and leader drop vertically, they will fall to the surface in soft waves.

At the end of the cast, the rod tip will be in this position, and the slack in the line and leader will ensure a drag-free drift.

Front View of the Roll Dump Cast

Begin the forward cast with the rod tilted slightly outward and in a vertical position.

Do not make a normal roll cast. Instead, sweep the rod through a longer speed-up-and-stop to make a larger than normal loop and then direct the rod tip to stop downward and short of the target.

This will cause the line to fall short of the target with the front of the line and the leader descending in a vertical manner.

The front portion of the line has fallen in soft waves and more of it continues to stack in waves, with the leader still coming down in a vertical manner.

As the cast nears the end, the leader falls in many soft waves.

You'll get a long drift with the leader and the front of the line in waves like this.

CHAPTER 8

Casts for Tight Quarters

A lot of times, the best places to fish are way back in the brush or under obstructions that most anglers can't, or don't bother to, reach. On brush-choked eastern brook trout streams, the best anglers have learned to deliver flies to fish with a host of creative casts that use a limited backcast. Bass and saltwater fish such as snook are ambush predators and make their living by hiding back in the brush waiting for the bait. To catch these fish consistently, you have to learn how to get your fly under overhanging brush, boat docks, and other types of cover. After you master some of these casts, you won't avoid those difficult-to-reach spots, but rather seek them out and enjoy their challenges—because that may be where the big one lives.

STEEPLE CAST

The steeple cast that has been used for many years involves making a backcast in the normal manner with an attempt to throw a vertical or near-vertical cast. The problem with this older steeple cast is that the rod tip invariably speeds up and stops in a slightly backward direction. The line will go in the direction the tip speeds up and stops, and all too often the fly snags in the trees. This steeple cast employs the principle that the line will go in the direction the rod tip speeds up and stops—so the mission is to stop the tip in a vertical direction that will clear the obstruction. This first sequence shows the steeple cast as it has been recommended for decades, but which often causes the fly to snag in vegetation behind the angler. With this cast you will also not be able to cast as well with tall obstructions behind you. If this is the case, use the following near-vertical cast.

Steeple Cast

Lower the rod tip until it touches the water.

Remove all slack and concentrate on making the highest backcast you can. Make sure your thumb is behind the handle, opposite the target.

When the line leaves the water, you can begin the backcast.

Delay the backcast speed-up-and-stop as long as you can.

Try to make the speed-up-and-stop vertically.

Even with a short speed-up-and-stop, some of the line's direction will be up and slightly back.

This will cause the backcast to travel behind you.

The line will continue to unroll behind.

The line remains high above the surface.

Before the line completely unrolls, begin the forward cast.

Hold the rod tip steady immediately after the speed-up-and-stop to allow the line to unroll toward the target.

Just before the line completely unrolls, begin to lower the rod.

Continue to lower the rod.

Before the fly touches the water, the rod should be in a fishing position.

NEAR-VERTICAL CAST

On small streams where there is not enough room for any normal backcast—even with a roll cast—the near-vertical cast is often the only answer. This cast is a useful modification of the steeple cast, where you would make a high enough backcast so that the line clears brush and other casting obstructions behind you.

When you make a near-vertical cast, you turn your hand and start your backcast with your thumb underneath the rod.

This way you can stop with the rod going straight and almost vertical. If you start with your thumb in this manner, you are able to better control where the fly is going to go—whether it is more or less straight back like the hole-in-trees cast (also called the Galway cast) or straight up as in the near-vertical cast. If you try this cast with your hand on top of the rod grip, like in the conventional steeple cast, your hand travels back toward what you want to avoid hitting.

Near-Vertical Cast

This is one of the few casts where your elbow does not stay on the shelf. Turn your hand so that your thumb is behind the handle from the direction the backcast is to be delivered. To aid in the cast, the rod needs a long stroke so the rod tip touches the water.

This close-up shows how to position your hands.

Begin the cast using a full arm stroke.

It is vital to make the speed-up-and-stop straight up. If the rod tip stops while going slightly backward, the line will go in that direction and tangle in the background bushes or trees.

Allow the line to unroll upward.

Just before the line completely unrolls, turn your rod hand around so you can make a forward cast.

Concentrate on speeding up and stopping the line parallel to the water. As the line unrolls toward the target, begin lowering the rod.

As the cast ends, the rod is in a fishing position.

AERIAL ROLL CAST

When I started trout fishing, I fished up in the Blue Ridge Mountains near my home in Maryland and close by in Pennsylvania where most of the streams are less than 25 feet wide. On these streams, because of the dense overhanging foliage, you were not only limited to what kind of space you had behind you, but also above you, which made casts like the steeple cast (where you make an extremely high backcast) impossible.

In tight quarters with no backcast room, I learned that I could load the rod by holding onto the hook and sweeping the rod straight up. When you bring the rod tip down to the water to begin the cast, the line on the water as you sweep the rod tip up loads the rod. I also learned that you needed to hold the hook by the bend in between your pointer finger and thumb so that you don't hook yourself with this cast. After going straight up with the rod, I could come down at an angle and make short casts into pockets that a lot of fishermen avoided because of the difficulty of fishing them.

If no more than the leader and 6 to 8 feet of fly line is needed to reach the target, you can be right up against the brush. The photos here illustrate about the maximum distance possible with this cast—about 25 feet.

> *When making the aerial roll, the fly line should be positioned on the water to the right of the rod, so that when you sweep the rod up, the line goes to the right of your casting arm and doesn't hit you.*

Aerial Roll Cast

Hold the hook between your thumb and finger so the point is exposed and directed away from you. This stops you from impaling yourself during the cast. Touch the rod tip to the water in the target's direction. The line tension on the water and the distance that you move the rod tip help load the rod. The fly line should be positioned on the water to the right of the rod, so that when you sweep the rod up, the line goes right of your casting arm and doesn't hit you.

Raise the rod rapidly in the opposite direction of the target.

Be sure to clench the hook firmly so the rod flexes against the fly held between your thumb and finger as it continues to sweep swiftly upward and back.

For maximum distance, this is about as far back as the rod should travel before stopping abruptly. If the structure is close behind, you will have to stop sooner. If you have held the fly firmly, the rod should be loaded.

With proper thumb/finger pressure, the speeding line will pull the fly free from your hand as the rod stops.

Begin the forward cast the moment the rod tip speeds up and stops. Note that all this time your elbow should remain on the imaginary shelf and your rod hand kept low. Elevating the elbow or hand reduces the cast's efficiency.

Sweep the rod forward toward the target. To get a quieter presentation, speed up and stop the tip in a direction well above the target. Slowly lower the rod after the stop. The cast should end with the rod low, causing the fly to quietly fall to the water.

HOLE-IN-TREES CAST

This is a similar cast to the near vertical, though you are directing the backcast behind you rather than vertically. On many streams, if you cast without looking behind you, you will almost certainly tangle the fly in the bushes. Look behind you for openings in the brush or get into a position where there is an opening behind you, and look at the hole as you make the cast. Like in the near-vertical cast, place your thumb under the rod handle so that you are casting toward the hole.

Though the cast has many freshwater applications, I learned this cast tarpon fishing, where I'd often be fishing on one side of the boat when the guide would yell, "Fish behind you!" If you turn around and make that backcast, just like you were throwing at a hole in the trees, you make this cast with accuracy. The key to making a distance cast like this (60 feet or so) is to not make the cast until the line leaves the water.

A lot of saltwater anglers will just present the cast on their backcast, which is okay for distance, but you really need to practice to be able to make an accurate presentation casting over your thumb (presenting on the backcast). People tend to twist their wrists when they do that—as they make the backcast, their knuckles are up and the rod grip is above the thumb. If you turn your thumb at all, you are going to make an inaccurate cast. The hole-in-trees cast (or back-forward cast, as I have called it in previous books) solves that problem.

Hole-in-Trees Cast

Face the hole in the bushes and lower the rod until the tip touches the water. Most important, you should raise your elbow and position your thumb behind the rod handle from the hole in the bushes. This is another cast where your elbow does not stay in contact with the shelf during the cast.

Accelerate your rod hand toward the hole.

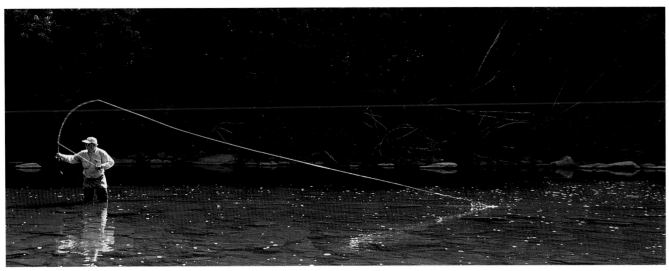

Continue to accelerate the rod, and your elbow will begin lowering—that's okay. When the line end leaves the surface of the water, make the shortest speed-up-and-stop you can in the direction of the hole in the trees.

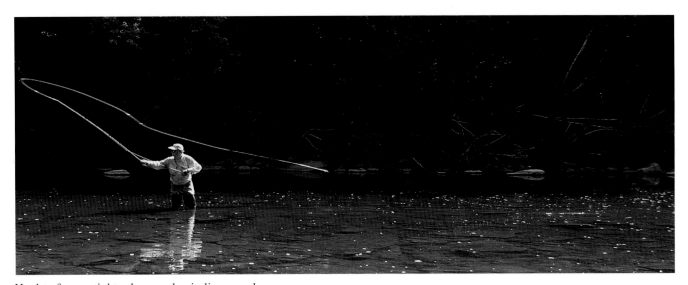

Haul to form a tighter loop and gain line speed.

Do not follow through by dipping the rod. This opens the loop, possibly making it too big to enter the hole.

As the line loop enters the hole, bring your rod hand around for the forward cast.

With the rod low, your elbow on the shelf, and your thumb behind the rod handle from the target, begin the forward cast.

Speed up and stop.

Aim high.

Don't lower the rod immediately.

Before the line loop unrolls, lower the rod to a fishing position.

Close-up of the Hole-in-Trees Cast

Your thumb is behind the handle from the target—the hole in the bushes. The rod tip touches the water to aid the cast. Elevate your elbow.

For accuracy, keep your thumb directly behind the handle from the target as you sweep the rod forward while hauling.

Anglers tend to direct their casts where they are looking. Concentrate on the hole in the bushes as the rod moves forward while constantly building line speed.

Concentrate on making the shortest speed-up possible to form the tightest loop that will penetrate the hole.

As the tight loop enters the hole, turn your rod hand around so your thumb is behind the handle from the next target—then cast to the fish.

Begin making a normal cast. If the cast is short (as here), little hauling is required, but on longer casts, the longer haul helps speed the line. Your elbow is now on the shelf and tracking forward.

Your arm stays on the shelf as a normal forward cast directs the line ahead.

Speed up and stop in the direction of the presentation and then lower to a fishing position.

SIDE ROLL CAST

This cast is useful in a wide variety of situations, from casting under bridges to casting under brush. If you want to make the cast go under the bushes and just 2 feet above the water, for instance, when you begin the speed-up-and-stop on your forward cast, it should stay parallel with the water's surface. If you don't, the loop isn't going to stay parallel to the water.

> *As you move the rod tip from a vertical to sidearm position on the side roll cast, don't pause. Make it one smooth and continuous motion. Speed up and stop parallel to the water.*

A lot of people, when they first try this cast, make the speed-up-and-stop in a downward direction. Bring the rod back vertically, or almost vertically, and then simply tilt the rod tip to the side and begin your forward cast. Don't stop when you move from a vertical to sidearm position or you will create slack in the line.

Side Roll Cast

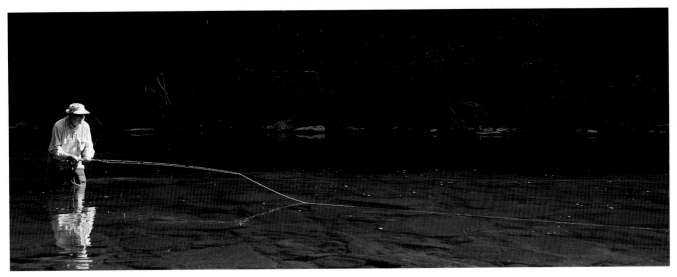

Begin as with any normal roll cast—with your elbow on the imaginary shelf, thumb behind the handle from the target, and hand low.

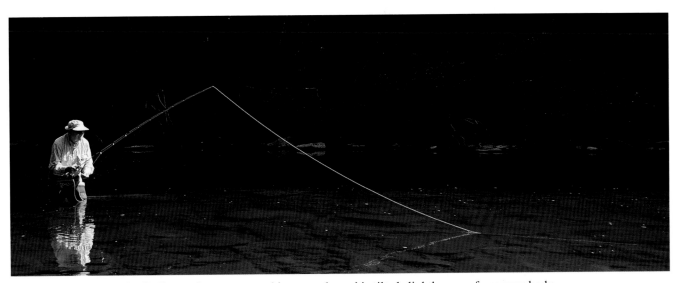

Raise the rod to draw the fly line end near you, making sure the rod is tilted slightly away from your body.

Continue to lift the rod tip.

When the line end is 10 feet or closer, allow the end to stop on the surface. Quickly lay the rod sideways toward the surface.

Continue to lower the rod, keeping your rod hand low and your thumb behind the rod handle away from the target.

Continue to lower the rod until it is parallel with the surface.

When the rod is parallel to the surface, begin the forward cast.

It is important to make the forward stroke and the speed-up-and-stop parallel to the surface. Your elbow stays on the imaginary shelf, your rod hand is low, and your thumb is behind the rod handle away from the target as the tip stops in the direction of the target.

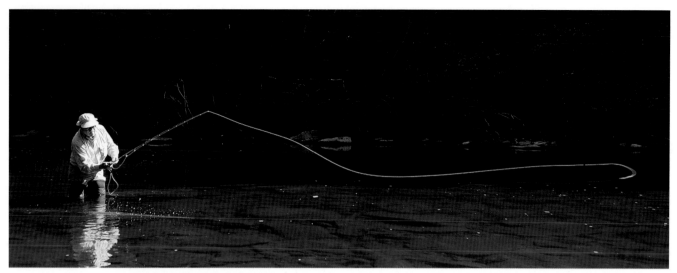

The line should unroll parallel to the surface.

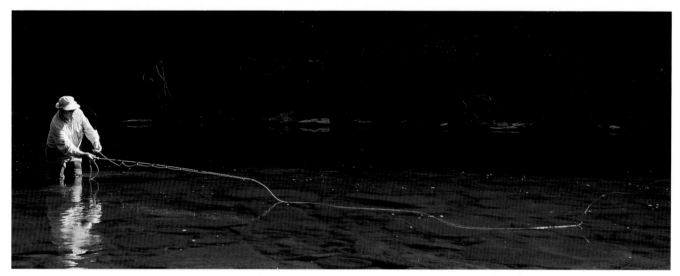

Just before the leader unrolls, lower the rod to a fishing position.

Rear View of the Side Roll Cast

Begin with your rod tip low.

Draw the line back with the rod tilted slightly away from your body, as with a normal roll cast.

Slowly raise the rod tip, keeping your elbow on the imaginary shelf and your rod hand low.

Continue to slowly raise the rod tip. Draw the end of the fly line until it is within 10 feet. When the line end stops, begin the side roll cast.

Dip the rod back a little, making sure the line still drapes away from the rod. Quickly lower the rod toward the surface.

Continue lowering the rod.

When the rod is parallel with the surface, begin the side roll cast. The elbow is on the shelf, the rod hand is low, and the thumb is behind the rod handle away from the target. Accelerate the rod forward and make a speed-up-and-stop. The shorter the speed-up-and-stop, the tighter the loop. If the line, leader, and fly are to roll sideways parallel to the surface, the forward casting stroke and speed-up-and-stop must be parallel to the surface. Too many anglers speed up and stop the tip in a slightly downward motion, which forces the line downward, and the unrolling leader catches in the overhanging structure.

If the stroke and speed-up-and-stop are parallel to the water, the loop will unroll parallel to the surface.

Allow the loop to unroll.

When the unrolling line loop nears the target, begin to lower the rod.

Continue lowering the rod.

Just before the line and leader completely unroll, the rod should be in a fishing situation.

TUNNEL ROLL CAST

Most trout streams are hard fished, and the places few people can cast a fly are some of the most productive spots to fish. That is one reason it is good to learn casting with either hand, since there are right- and left-hand holes best fished with one hand or the other. One of the places on a small stream where few people can present a fly is in a narrow pool overhung with vegetation. I call this a tunnel. Rarely does someone cast well up into these tunnels, and smart trout have learned to live there. The tunnel roll will let you fish as far as 20 feet into such vegetative tunnels. Sometimes you need to make a cast close to water so that you can fish under overhanging bushes, a bridge, a boat dock, etc. Though this cast is hard to make at long distances (it is effective to about 45 feet), it allows you to fish flies in places where others can't.

Turn the rod to the side to avoid hitting the small wire hook keeper when you slam the rod with your cupped hand.

By coming forward low to the water and slamming the rod against the hand, you make the best stop that you possibly can, which creates a tight loop and sends the fly and line tight under the bushes. I rarely make this kind of cast with a vertical rod, because I generally use it to get under something. I try to tilt the rod as far to the right as possible to get the rod tip as low as possible to the water. Because of the force with which you slam the bottom of the rod, this cast is not advisable with bamboo rods.

Notice that in this sequence, instead of slowly drawing the line back as in a regular roll cast, I lift it out of the water slightly to throw more line behind me with ease. This is similar to the switch cast. You can make this cast by slowly drawing the line back behind you, but that can limit the distance you are able to cast because you can draw the line back only so far.

Tunnel Roll Cast

The goal is to unroll a line just above the surface. The more you crouch and the closer you can make your rod hand travel to the surface, the lower the cast can travel. Kneeling is best. Begin with the line taut and the rod low and pointed at the target.

Begin raising the rod. As with all roll casts, the rod should be tilted slightly to the side to make sure the line doesn't tangle on the forward cast. Bring the rod slowly back, keeping your elbow and hand low—the lower the better. Raising your hand will prevent the line from unrolling into the tunnel. The line is trapped under the rod handle, and your line hand is free.

As you elevate your rod hand, the rod is drawing the line end closer. Cup your other hand, and hold it out just above the reel.

When the line end is within 10 feet, the rod should be tilted to the side and slightly behind. Make an easy circular backcast so that the line end falls close to you. Keep the rod hand as low as possible while bringing the rod tip back. Cup your line hand in front of the lowest part of the rod blank.

Slam the rod on the forward cast against your other hand on the stop. It is important to turn the reel outward as shown. This places the ring keeper just above your rod hand and off to the side. If the reel isn't turned, the ring keeper could strike and injure your hand.

With the D loop behind you, begin the forward cast. Cup your line hand, and hold it low and just above the height of the reel. Your elbow should be as low to the water as possible, and your rod hand travels in a straight path toward the target.

Accelerate the rod rapidly forward, and at the end of the cast, slam the rod against your hand, making sure not to hit the hook keeper.

This close-up shows the acceleration of the rod.

Striking the rod against your line hand with your elbow and rod tip low develops an incredibly tight and fast traveling loop that will go well up into a small tunnel.

Don't lower the rod tip after you strike the rod with your hand—you want to maintain the tightest loop and straightest line possible so the fly can reach the target.

Just before the line completes unrolling, lower the rod and be ready to fish.

SKIP CAST

Homer Rhodes was a legendary Florida guide and former game warden who lived in a houseboat on Barren River near Everglades City, Florida. In the late 1960s, we would fish for snook together in small creeks in the backcountry. Snook lie just back under the mangroves, particularly on higher tides, and then sweep out and grab any prey that swims by. They are a lot like largemouth bass, but with an attitude—they strike harder, fight better, and are faster. The key to catching snook is to get your fly close to or back under the mangroves. In those small creeks, we used short, 7-foot rods with 9- or 10-weight lines so that we could load them at short distances, just as small-stream trout anglers often overline their rods to load the rod easier. We needed a way to drive the fly under the mangroves, and the skip cast, in some situations, is the only way that you can get your fly in there.

The skip cast is also a very effective method to fish docks. We used to fish a lot of docks at night. In Florida, almost all of the docks have lights on them that attract small baitfish such as little glass minnows, which in turn attract snook, baby

Begin the forward cast at a slightly upward or parallel angle to the water. If you come forward with the rod tip traveling down, you can't skip the line and fly.

tarpon, ladyfish, and other species. Fishing under the lights is popular these days, but back then it wasn't. The greatest night of fishing that I had was when the Miami Dolphins were in the Super Bowl and everyone in Florida was watching the football game, except for me and Captain Jim Grace. Every dock we visited was hot. As we approached each one, we could see bait spraying in the air—sure signs they were being chased by hungry snook. We fished maybe three-quarters of the night, and it was one of the greatest fishing experiences of my life.

The key to making a good skip cast is to think about skipping a stone. To skip a flat stone, you throw it to hit the water close to you, and after it hits the water, the stone stays low to the water as it skips. Come back as low to the water as possible (while still trying to go back on an upward angle), and then come forward with a lot of line speed parallel to a slightly upward angle. If you come forward at a downward angle, the fly and line won't skip. Weighted flies work the best with this cast, but you can do it with all flies.

Skip Cast

You need to make this cast from the side. Start with the rod low to the water.

When the line end leaves the water, make a low backcast with your elbow on the shelf and your thumb behind the rod hand away from the target. This is a very difficult cast to make if you come back vertically.

By the end of the backcast, make sure the rod is well behind you.

Just before the backcast completely unrolls, begin the forward cast.

Direct the forward cast slightly downward.

Keep the rod tip low to the water, and develop a lot of line speed by hauling.

Aim the speed-up-and-stop so the fly line end strikes the water just in front of you.

The line will hit the water and skip toward the target.

After the line skips on the water, it remains close to the surface and will sneak under overhanging structure.

Near the end of the cast, lower the rod to begin your retrieve.

TIGHT QUARTERS CAST

This cast is especially helpful in the East where some of the best trout water is brush-choked. Even when fishing on small streams, I like to use longer rods because they help make better roll casts, are easier to mend, and the extra length helps me get better drifts. But you frequently encounter situations

> *The less you use the rod to help make the cast, the faster you have to haul.*

where you don't have enough room to cast with a longer rod. I figured out that I could put 2 feet of rod behind me and instantly convert my 9-foot rod to a 7-foot one. Place the lower portion of the rod behind you and brace it with your body throughout the entire cast. Hauling really helps on this cast.

Tight Quarters Cast

Position the rod behind your body, tucked under your arm. You will brace the rod with your body through the entire cast. With your rod hand, grasp the rod above the handle on the blank. The spot where you grip the rod determines the rod length used in casting. Since there is no handle to grip, you need to place your finger along the rod blank.

To make the cast, you must swivel your body while the rod tucked under your arm remains immobile. A double haul helps. Your body motion combined with a haul make the cast. Press your arm firmly against the rod to hold it in position, and rotate your upper body while making a short haul to get a good tight backcast.

Keep the rod clenched against your body while further rotating your upper body and hauling.

As the backcast ends, your body should have pivoted 90 degrees. This causes the backcast to unroll in a tight loop. You are making the cast by just rotating your body and hauling.

Slide your haul hand back toward the rod butt to eliminate slack, and begin to rotate your upper body back to make the forward cast.

During the forward cast, pivot your body back in the other direction and haul on the line. Be sure to stop dead with the rod.

Continue to pivot to the front and haul on the line.

Note that as the cast ends, the rod portion tucked under your arm has not moved through the entire cast. This method enables you to throw incredibly tight loops into tight quarters.

RIGHT-ANGLE CAST

I developed this cast on small eastern streams, where brush frequently grows down to the water. Wading along the shoreline, I would often need to cast at right angles to the brush at my back to get the fly out in the middle of the stream. Because I knew that once I got the line moving I could make a cast, and that the line was going to go in the direction that I sped up and stopped, I discovered that I could make a cast parallel to the bank and then speed up and stop out toward where I wanted the line to go. This cast is only effective to about 25 feet.

Right-Angle Cast

Lower the rod tip to the surface. Keep your thumb behind the rod away from the target and your elbow on the shelf.

Draw the rod back parallel to the streambank.

When the line end leaves the water, make a backcast parallel to the bank.

Try to throw a tight, fast line loop with a short speed-up-and-stop on the backcast.

As soon as the rod stops on the backcast, begin moving the rod forward parallel to the streambank, which will load the rod.

When the rod is vertical, turn your hand so your thumb is behind the handle away from the target area.

Immediately begin a forward cast toward the target.

Make sure the rod tip stops straight ahead. Many anglers tend to speed up and stop in a downward direction.

The line will change direction and head toward the target. Note that your elbow remains on the shelf throughout the cast.

When the line unrolls well away from the tip, begin to lower the rod.

As the fly nears the target, lower the rod to a fishing position.

CHANGE-OF-DIRECTION CAST

One of the most common situations where you need to make a change-of-direction cast is after the line drifts downstream and you want to cast it quickly back upstream. Or you may be fishing to a feeding trout when suddenly one rises in another direction. Though this cast isn't as applicable to tight quarters as some of the other casts in this section—you need to have room behind you—I include it here because it uses similar principles as the change-of-direction cast with no backcast room. Many Spey casts are designed to make similar changes of direction, but this one only requires knowing the basic casting motions and can help those who might not know or might not want to use Spey casts. I use this for short casts (15–20 feet), and for longer casts, I usually use a variation of the snake roll (see page 263).

Change-of-Direction Cast

Lower the rod to within inches of the surface.

Sweep the rod close to the water upstream.

Continue sweeping the rod in the direction of the cast while beginning to turn so you will be facing the target.

Keep sweeping the rod along the surface until it points at the target. It is important to keep the rod tip as close to the surface as possible. Fight the tendency to elevate the rod as you sweep it along. By keeping the tip as low to the surface as possible, you maximize the length of the backcast stroke. You should now be facing the target. Without pausing after the sweep of the rod, make a slightly rounded motion of the rod tip and then accelerate directly away from the target. A short haul on the line helps. Do not elevate your elbow (a common mistake), as this will open the line loop and cause you to lose line speed on the backcast.

Make the speed-up-and-stop directly away from the target.

The backcast will flow opposite the target.

Make sure you wait for the line to unroll behind you.

Just before the line unrolls on the backcast, begin the forward cast. Keep your elbow on the shelf throughout this cast.

Speed up and stop the rod toward the target.

Allow the loop to unroll away from the rod tip before beginning to lower it. Before the fly reaches the target area, lower the rod.

CHAPTER 9

Picking Up Line

S urface tension holds a floating line to the water's surface, and it is important to not rip it from the water, alerting fish. You have to bring sinking
lines close to or on the surface to make a backcast, and whenever you pick
up a line, the best possible backcast is directed opposite the target. You will catch
more fish by learning to pick up line efficiently with different tackle and in different fishing situations.

Sometimes the standard pickup doesn't do the best job, and you want to be
able to pick up a fly more quietly, or need to pick up a fly that has a lot of grass on
it. For these situations, you have to make some more specialized casts.

ROLL CAST PICKUP

You should never pick up a dry fly or a popping bug until all the line is off the
water. If you rip line free of the surface of the water, you can make a lot of splash
that alerts fish. The roll cast pickup lifts the line more or less vertically from the
water and doesn't spook fish. This cast also flushes more water from the fly and
line, preventing a lot of water spray when you make a forward cast.

In trout fishing, one of the places that the roll cast pickup works very well is
in the tail of a pool. If you are fishing a dry fly and the line is drifting back and
might be swept over the edge of pool into the next pool, making a quick roll
pickup lifts the fly almost vertically, and you don't make a lot of noise. You can't
make a conventional pickup because you tend to be raising your rod tip as the fly
drifts back toward you. The roll cast pickup also works well on calm pools to quietly lift the line, leader, and fly without alarming wise fish.

Popping bugs can make loud fish-alerting noises when lifted for a backcast. If
you pick some cupped-face popping bugs or deer-hair flies such as the Letort Hop-
per off the water in the conventional manner, the line that is still on the water tends
to pull them forward instead of up and creates disturbance on the water. The roll
cast pickup lifts the fly vertically out of the water, which eliminates this problem.

Roll Cast Pickup

Start the cast with the rod tip almost in the water, pointing toward the target.

Tilt the rod slightly away from your body, and begin drawing the line close by elevating the rod. Raising the rod will quietly lift line free of the surface.

Continue drawing the line. You cannot make a backcast until all line is above the surface.

Move the rod behind your body, and continue drawing line.

When the line end is within 10 feet, stop drawing the rod and line back.

Accelerate the rod and make a high forward cast. Keep your elbow on the shelf and your rod hand low.

In the final moment of the cast, speed up and stop the tip to get a climbing cast. The shorter and faster the speed-up-and-stop, the tighter the loop and the more efficient the cast.

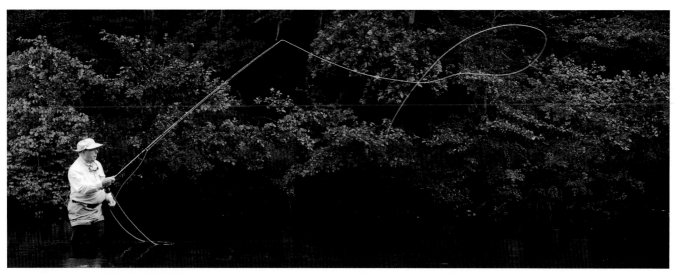

When you speed up and stop the tip, do not lower the rod. The unrolling line loop will begin to pull the leader and fly vertically from the water.

As the line unrolls, it continues to lift the leader and fly.

The unrolling line will begin to straighten the leader. Once the fly is above the surface, you can make a backcast without creating a lot of disturbance on the surface of the water.

The moment the leader unrolls, begin the backcast.

During the backcast, your elbow remains on the imaginary shelf and your rod hand travels back in a straight plane.

At the end of the backcast, begin a normal forward cast.

While accelerating forward, keep your elbow on the shelf and your rod hand moving directly ahead on the speed-up-and-stop.

Begin to lower the rod tip after the line is well away from it.

Don't lower it too fast or you will pull open the loop.

Continue to slowly lower the rod tip.

If the speed-up-and-stop was brief and directed straight ahead and you did not lower the rod tip too soon, most of the fly line will be straight and aimed at the target.

Before the fly touches down, the rod should be in a fishing position.

SNAKE ROLL VARIATIONS

The snake roll is a Spey cast used to change directions, usually after a drifting retrieve, and allows the angler to quickly roll cast to the target. The snake roll is now used by many Spey casters rather than using the double Spey cast. The snake roll variation is not a roll cast but employs the same casting technique, and is useful for quickly changing directions, up to about 100 degrees on the cast, in a matter of seconds. This works great if you are fishing on one side of the boat and suddenly a bonefish appears on the other side. Normally the guide would want to reposition the boat so that you wouldn't hit him with the cast, but you can make this cast and not make the guy on the poling platform nervous. If a trout suddenly rises in the opposite direction of where you are fishing, you can quickly get the fly to the fish. At the end of a drift with a dry fly, you don't have to make several false casts to get the fly back upstream. You can use this snake roll variation to be fishing again with a single backcast.

With a lot of line on the water, you need to make two tight circles with the rod tip, rather than one.

Because you can only make a cast after the line end moves, you can twirl the rod tip in a tight circle (but not draw it back toward you) to get the line moving and make the cast. In any efficient cast, the backcast should be 180 degrees from the target, so if you want to change direction from right to left, twirl to the right to line the rod up opposite the target to make a good back and forward cast. With more line on the water for longer pickups, you need to make two twirls—the first to get the line moving and the second to get the line off the water. The tighter that you make the twirls, the less slack that is in the line when you make the backcast.

Snake Roll to the Left

To quickly change direction from the right to the left, lower the rod to remove all slack from the line. Then quickly raise it to lift as much line from the water as possible.

Continue raising the rod tip.

When all the line has been lifted from the water (ensuring a quiet backcast), rotate the rod tip in a tight circle. If you don't have much line on the water, you only need to make a single, small twirl. If a lot of line is on the water, then you need two twirls to get the line off the surface. All line should be lifted from the water before you make the cast. Do not draw back on the rod tip; this pulls the line toward you and makes a poor cast. If the change-of-direction cast is to be to the left, the rod tip must twirl to the right (the opposite direction). If the forward cast is made to the right, the rod tip must twirl to the left.

With the short line, make a single, swift, tight twirl with the elevated rod tip, lifting all the line quietly from the surface.

Make the cast to the left. By twirling the rod once to the right, the backcast travels opposite the target.

As the backcast unrolls, face the target.

Keep your elbow on the shelf as you begin the forward cast.

Note how far forward of my body my casting arm is. Moving the rod the greatest distance possible before the speed-up-and-stop loads the rod deeply.

Speed up and stop the rod toward the target. Lower the rod as the line unrolls forward.

This swift change of direction requires only a few seconds.

Snake Roll to the Right

To make a change of direction to the right, twirl the rod tip once or twice to the left. The biggest reason that people tend to botch this cast is that they do not turn and face their target when they make the forward cast.

If you are fishing to the left, begin a change of direction to the right by raising the rod tip to lift as much line as possible from the surface.

This line is short, so you can twirl the elevated rod once to the left (opposite the direction of the forward cast). If a long line were on the water, you would need two twirls to lift all line from the surface.

The shock produced by the tight twirl begins lifting the line from the surface.

The single twirl to the left positions the rod behind you, and the line is moving opposite the target on the backcast.

It is important for a right-handed caster to now turn his body to the right, face the target, and start a smooth forward cast. A left-handed caster, when changing direction from right to left, needs to swivel his body to the left to face the target. Not turning to face the target is the main reason anglers have trouble with this cast. They continue to face the direction they started the cast.

When first learning this cast, many anglers tend to throw the line downward, but it should be aimed well above the water to allow the cast to unroll to the target.

Lower the rod as the cast is delivered to the target. The change from left to right has been made in seconds.

Inefficient Snake Roll

If you start the cast with the rod held too high, you won't be able to lift the line properly. Making twirls that are too big creates large waves in the line that have to be removed before the rod can move the fly on the backcast. Such large waves also strike the water and could alert the fish. Pulling the rod back as it is twirled also creates unwanted slack. The rod tip should stay the same distance from you at the beginning and end of the twirling motions.

I begin lifting the rod and line but am drawing the rod back toward myself, which will produce unwanted slack that has to be removed before a cast can be made. The rod tip moves in wide circles while the line is still on the surface. A correct technique is to use the rod to lift as much line as possible from the water before twirling the rod. If not, the line is ripped from the surface on the backcast, alerting fish nearby.

The rod begins to form a large circle. The rod should be raised much higher.

There is a large, circling shock wave in the line. The rod rotating low to the water results in a bad snake roll.

The large wave introduces slack that must be removed before making the backcast. If I make a low, wide circling motion, the line will strike the surface, producing a fish-alerting disturbance.

The large, circling shock wave throws the forward end of the fly down to the surface. I must now make the backcast and rip the line from the water, creating more disturbance. The wide loops created by widely circling the rod tip develop a lot of slack that also make a backcast more difficult.

RIDDING GRASS CAST

When retrieving a fly in grassy, weedy, or leafy areas—in fresh or salt water—any piece of grass that catches on your fly can spoil the retrieve. Worse, you can't make another cast until you remove the grass or leaf. This usually entails bringing the fly to hand, removing the grass and taking time before making another cast, which frequently spells a lost opportunity. I stumbled on this technique while fishing for largemouth bass, where I would constantly catch vegetation on my poppers and subsurface flies. Since then, it has proved invaluable everywhere I fish, whether for bonefish or trout.

You can remove grass from your line and fly with several methods. As you raise the line, you can shake the rod tip and make a bunch of vertical shock waves, and then when the line jumps out of the water, you can make a backcast with the fly still underwater. A much easier and more controlled way to rid your fly of grass is to make a low roll cast with a short, tight loop, and the moment the line is out of the water—but all the leader is still in the water—make a hard backcast and haul. The water holds onto the weeds, and the hook shears through the weeds as it flies back. You only have to remove the toughest weeds by hand.

I've had a number of occasions in fresh and salt water where I noticed grass on a fly that a fish was following. I knew that the fish would never take the fly with the grass on it, so I picked it up and recast using this technique. Within seconds, I'd have a grass-free fly back in action in front of the fish.

Ridding Grass Cast

While you are retrieving the fly, you notice grass or a leaf on the fly. Lower the rod tip nearly to the surface.

Draw the rod back low.

Continue to draw the rod back so that it is behind you.

Begin making a roll cast.

Make a roll cast directed parallel with the water. Try to aim the line at the nail knot. You want a tight loop with little slack in the line.

As the line unrolls forward, focus on where the leader and the fly should be.

Concentrate on the unrolling loop, and recognize when all line is out of the water.

When all of the fly line has been lifted out of the water but the leader and fly remain underwater, make a fast backcast.

The high-speed backcast (a fast, single haul often helps) rips the leader swiftly from the water, and the fly knifes through the grass.

Just before the backcast unrolls completely, make a forward cast. With the grass or leaf removed, you can present the fly to the fish.

Loose Line Pickup

When loose line lies on the water in front of you, such as when you change flies and drop the fly, leader, and some line on the water, you can use this technique to quickly cast as much as 20 feet of line and leader on the water without stripping in the line. Once you move the end of the fly line in wide figure-eight loops, you can make the cast.

Loose line lies on the surface in front of you, often after you have just replaced your fly. Lower the rod tip close to the surface, and move the rod widely to the side. Never stop the rod as it sweeps back and forth.

Sweep the rod tip in the opposite direction. Don't make short sweeps or the line may tangle.

As the line moves toward the rod, elevate it. Continuously move the rod in wide figure-eight motions with the tip. Do not make short motions or the line may tangle. Make wide figure-eight motions as shown here.

Without stopping, sweep the tip in the opposite direction while keeping the rod tip high.

Immediately return the rod in the opposite direction while lowering the rod slightly to prepare for the best possible backcast.

Repeat the rod sweeping motion. The rod should never stop moving until the backcast.

Watch the line end while sweeping the rod back and forth. Anytime the line end begins moving, you can make the backcast in the opposite direction of the target.

Allow the backcast to almost straighten before starting the forward cast.

Accelerate forward and speed up and stop toward the target.

Lower the rod to a fishing position.

CHAPTER 10

Wind Casts

Anglers working the beaches almost always have an inshore wind, as air over the cooler seas moves toward the warmer land. Big-river fishermen seeking steelhead and salmon constantly battle wind, as do trout anglers fishing light lines on Western rivers. Many bonefish, tarpon, and redfish are lost because the wind blew the fly off target. Yet, wind can be your friend. The wind ruffles the surface and disguises imperfect casts, whereas on a calm surface the fish would have spooked. With a good wind at your back, you can cast more line than the store sold you.

Because you need more line speed on either the back or forward cast, a good double haul is essential to defeat the breeze. If the wind is blowing hard, consider fishing a sinking line or a shooting head, which will generally be easier to cast than a floating line.

The following sequences cover when the wind is on your right side, when the wind is behind you, and when the wind is in front of you. When the wind is on your left, you don't have to worry about anything other than accuracy, and you can use your normal casting stroke. All the wind-casting sequences are for right-handed casters.

WIND ON RIGHT

When the wind is blowing toward your casting arm, it can blow the fly into you or tangle your cast. To prevent the line and fly from hitting you, make a sidearm cast with a full arm extension, and as you come forward, tilt the rod to the down-wind side of you. You don't need to tilt a lot, because the wind will blow the line and fly to the other side of you. Many anglers are taught to cast cross arm, but this restricts your casting motion, and you can't get any distance with this cast. If the wind is blowing really hard to your casting arm, turn around and present the fly on your backcast, or use the hole-in-trees cast.

Wind on Right

If the wind is blowing toward your rod hand, lower the rod and remove all slack.

Make a sidearm cast with the rod traveling low on the backcast.

If you make a backcast well to the side, the wind cannot blow the line or fly at you.

Make a normal forward cast by bringing the rod to a vertical position. The advantage of this cast is that you employ a longer forward stroke than you would with a restricted cross-body cast.

Just before the speed-up-and-stop, make sure the rod is tilted slightly to the left of you.

On the speed-up-and-stop, direct the line slightly to your downwind side.

In a strong wind, you don't need to the tilt the rod. If you bring it forward vertically, the stiff breeze will carry the fly harmlessly to the downwind side.

The line stays out of harm's way as the line unrolls forward.

The cast ends with no problem from the breeze.

WIND AT BACK

This wind allows you to cast the entire fly line, and then some, as long as you can make a good, tight backcast low to the water (or beach). To prepare for this type of situation, refine your backcast so that it travels low and straight or climbing slightly, the loops are tight, and there is no sag. Once you can do this, simply make a low, fast backcast into the wind, and then come forward high with a relatively open loop, shooting line, and let the wind take your line out like a kite.

Wind at Back

If the wind is behind you, it is difficult to make a backcast. Fortunately the wind won't hinder your forward cast. Begin the cast with the rod tip low and pointing at the fly.

Start the backcast with your thumb behind the rod handle away from the target and your elbow remaining on the shelf. Draw the line back with the rod.

It is important to make a tight loop on the backcast to penetrate the breeze.

You almost always need to double haul to properly unroll the line into the teeth of the wind. The stiffer the wind, the faster you should haul. It is important to throw the line low on the backcast, making sure the rod is held low, too. The higher the rod's position at the end of the backcast, the more difficult it is to throw a high forward cast.

Note that after the haul on the backcast, you need to reposition your line hand to just in front of the reel before the forward cast. The cast needs to be high. The lower the backcast, the easier it is to make a high forward cast.

Come forward, aiming high. Stop the rod, directing the tip skyward.

The purpose of throwing a high forward cast is to allow the wind to act on the line as if the line were a kite. In a strong wind, if you made a good backcast and an elevated forward cast, the wind could let you throw more line than you bought.

After the speed-up-and-stop, you can begin to shoot additional line.

WIND IN FRONT

If the wind is blowing into your face, make a high backcast and a forward cast with a tight loop aimed directly at the surface of the water—exactly the opposite of the cast that you make when the wind is behind you. In these conditions, you not only have to worry about punching your cast into the wind, but you also have to worry about accuracy, because as your leader unrolls, the wind will blow your fly off course. This is not a delicate cast because you are aiming right at the water, but there's generally enough chop on the water that presentation isn't as much of a factor.

> *To overcome a wind in your face, don't try to use extra force. Focus on making a tight loop and higher line speed. The rod hand should form the tight loop after accelerating the rod, and the haul speed should be increased.*

A good double haul helps make your line travel faster and decreases loop size, which helps when casting into a wind. Smaller loops are less air-resistant. The tendency when casting into the wind is to overpower the cast, which actually often opens the loop; instead, focus on hauling faster, not casting harder, to make narrow loops.

Other tricks to defeat a wind blowing in your face are to decrease the size of your flies or try to use less wind-resistant ones. Bulky deer-hair poppers, for instance, don't travel as well in a breeze as small, heavily weighted Clouser Minnows. Shorten your leader as much as conditions allow.

If possible, use a shooting head. The diameter and the line's material are important, especially when you need a distance cast. Anyone who has cast into the wind with a number 11 floating line and then a number 11 sinking line understands that the larger the line diameter, the more air resistance. It is better to fish with an intermediate or, better, a sinking line that has a smaller diameter than a floating line and is weighted.

Wind in Front

With the wind blowing at you, make a slightly elevated backcast.

Just before the line unrolls, begin the forward cast. The angle of the forward cast is not directed above the surface as normal but is aimed downward.

Because the wind is against you, it helps to haul—the longer the acceleration, the longer and faster the haul. Generate the line speed required to penetrate the wind with the hauling hand.

If the rod hand controls the loop size and the direction of the cast and you develop speed by hauling, then you maintain a tight and high-speed loop. Almost all anglers exert extra force with the rod hand when casting into the wind, and this deforms the loop and wastes energy.

Direct the fly toward the surface and at the target.

The fly enters the water the instant the leader straightens, so it has no chance to be blown back by the wind.

A straight cast has been made into the breeze, and you are ready to retrieve the fly.

SIDE WIND ACCURACY

Wind blowing from the side not only can affect the casting stroke, but it also blows the line and fly off target and for many anglers spoils the accuracy of the cast. This cast will deliver the fly on or close to the target in all but the worst side wind. Once you stop the rod tip, you cannot change the direction of the line's flight. Make a tight loop and high-speed cast directed at the surface. As soon as you stop the rod tip, lay all the line in the water by dropping the rod tip. Placing the line on the water prevents it from being blown around.

Side Wind Accuracy

The forward cast begins.

You need a high-speed forward cast: Accelerate the rod faster and increase haul speed to accomplish this.

Just as when casting into the wind, bring the rod well forward.

The speed-up-and-stop is in the direction of the surface target. The line will go in the direction the rod tip stops or straightens, so aim where you want the fly to enter the water.

Aim the fly down toward the surface.

Once the rod tip speeds up and stops, the direction of the cast has been determined and cannot be changed. Immediately after the stop, drop the rod tip to the surface. Because you have aimed the line and fly at the target and placed all line immediately in the water, it can't be blown sideways.

The cast is not blown off target, and you are ready to retrieve.

CHAPTER 11

Weighted Flies and Lines

The casts in this section cover casts for both fresh and salt water. Freshwater trout anglers most often fish leaders, sometimes long ones, with several split shot and one or two weighted nymphs. Some anglers cast sinking tip lines. Saltwater anglers typically fish with shooting heads. When casting any sort of weight, you need to modify your stroke to avoid tangles. Any extra weight amplifies the principle that the line goes in the direction you speed up and stop, so you can use this to your advantage to throw curves in the line or prevent that troubling hook with weighted flies that thwarts many anglers' fly-casting accuracy.

> *For the greatest tuck, use a long leader with a heavily weighted fly, and stop the rod tip high after a fast acceleration.*

TUCK CASTS

George Harvey, as far as I know, invented the tuck cast, which is a great example of how you can modify the basic fly cast to solve fly-casting problems. If you cast with the line and leader fairly straight as the fly drifts downstream, the current tends to loft the fly so it doesn't sink deep enough. Harvey discovered that he could tuck the sinking fly back under the line at the end of the cast to create slack and sink the fly faster. Because the fly is now downstream from a portion of the forward end of the line, the fly

can sink until the current pulls all slack from the leader and line. This allows the fly to dive deeper before a retrieve begins. Most people think the tuck is a useful tool for nymphs only, but it is just as effective when fishing streamers to get them deeper in the water column during the drift or retrieve.

The weighted fly and long leader coupled with high line speed cause the tuck, which is why it is almost impossible to make a good tuck cast with a dry fly or a very short leader. When you stop the rod just past vertical, the weighted fly is going so fast that it ducks down, but the tip of the rod snapping back causes the tuck. To get the maximum tuck, overcast your target, stopping the rod tip high enough so that the leader and fly have enough time to duck under the line. Many anglers, besides not stopping the rod tip sharply enough, cast too low on the forward cast and do not give the leader and fly time to duck under the line.

Some recommend that when you make this cast you should pull back on the rod tip, but I don't think that is necessary, and it also pulls out a lot of slack in the line that you wanted to put there in the first place. Also, this motion tends to rob the cast of accuracy.

Front Tuck Cast

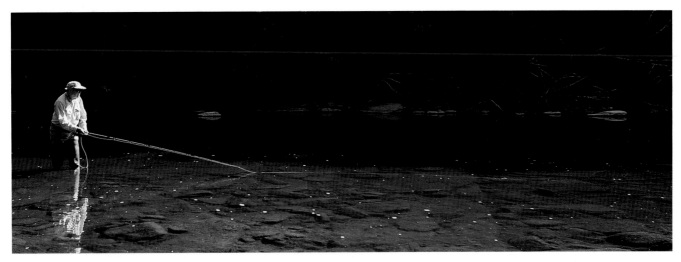

Start with the rod tip near the surface.

Raise the rod to begin the backcast.

When the fly line leaves the water, make the backcast.

Keep your elbow on the imaginary shelf and your thumb behind the rod handle away from the target throughout the cast.

Allow the backcast line to almost unroll.

Begin the forward cast, hauling to generate more line speed. Cast farther than your target.

Make a high cast that will allow the leader and fly to sweep under the fly line.

The more vertically the rod speeds up and stops, the greater the potential for a good tuck. If the line is aimed low to the water, there is no room for the fly to tuck under.

The cast goes well beyond the target. As the line unrolls and the weighted fly sweeps forward, the rod tip flexes downward. At this point, don't lower the rod. Stop the rod dead to allow the tip to flip the tuck into the cast. When the rod tip flexes back straight, it jerks the weighted fly back, tucking it and the leader underneath the line as it all falls to the surface.

The tip has flipped back and begins tugging the fly and leader back.

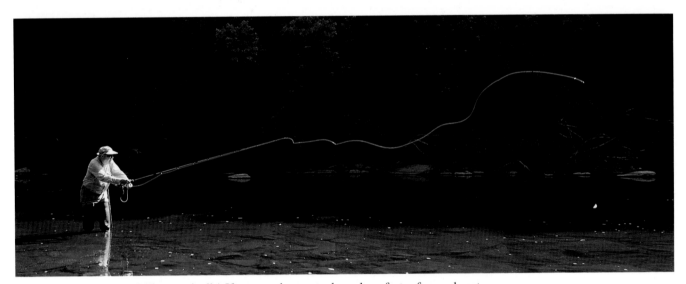

The leader and line are falling vertically. If you need more tuck, make a faster forward cast.

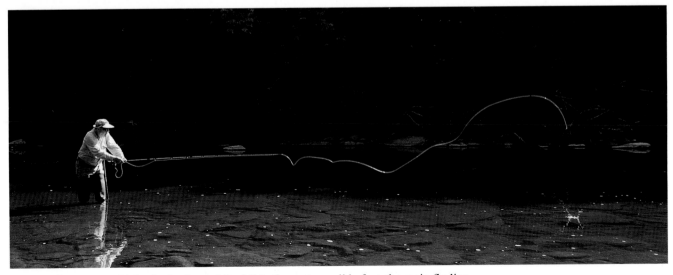

Because the cast was high, the leader and fly fall to the water well before the main fly line.

As the line hits the water, there is a lot of slack in the leader.

The fly continues to sink deeply because the slack in the leader isn't pulled out by the fly line.

Front View of the Front Tuck Cast

Begin the cast by pointing the rod toward the target with the tip close to the water.

Make a backcast as soon as the line end leaves the water.

Lift the rod to draw the line closer and get the end of the line moving.

The backcast should travel directly away from the target.

The backcast begins just before the line unrolls.

Stop the rod just past vertical. Do not follow through, and bring the rod to a dead stop.

Aim the forward cast high above the water so the leader and fly have enough room to tuck beneath the main fly line at the end of the cast. The forward cast should travel rapidly and go farther than the target to compensate for the tuck. A fast haul helps.

The line is traveling at a high speed with a weighted fly that would normally go well beyond the target.

Because the rod is vertical and rock steady, the fast-traveling line unrolls and flexes the rod tip downward. If you hold the rod still when the tip recoils or straightens, the weighted fly and some of the line will flip back toward you as it falls to the water. It is the recoiling of the rod tip that creates the tuck cast, causing the weighted fly and leader to flip underneath the main line.

The leader and the fly have curved underneath the main line, creating the desired slack. The weighted fly and leader are tucked under the fly line and are sinking as the current begins to pull the fly line downstream.

Curve Tuck Casts

The fly goes in the direction you stop the rod tip. It is possible to accurately throw a curve to the left by casting in a vertical position and speeding up and stopping at an angle to the target, which flexes the rod tip and throws a curve to the left.

With a side tuck, you can place additional line upstream when fishing across the current and get the fly deeper. A tuck cast curved to the left can be an advantage for getting a better drift in some fishing situations. Let's say you are walking up the center of a 30-foot-wide stream and the fish are holding on the left bank. If you make a regular tuck cast, the line is going to go down; if you tuck the line to the left, you are throwing a curve and a tuck, and you'll get the fly much deeper in the water.

Tuck Cast (Left Curve)

Begin with the rod tip low to the water. Your elbow will stay on the imaginary shelf and your thumb behind the rod handle away from the target. Tilt the rod slightly away from your body, and raise it to draw the line toward you. When the line end leaves the water, make the backcast.

Elevate the rod slightly and begin the forward cast before the line end unrolls. Make a high and very fast forward cast using a haul to help.

Tilt the rod tip and stop the rod just past vertical on the forward cast.

The high speed of the cast and the weighted fly combined with the speed-up-and-stop to the left throws the fly in a curve to the left. Aim the cast slightly up. Do not follow through, but stop the rod dead and hold it there. This causes the rod tip to flex to the left, throwing a curve in the line.

Because the cast is high and has more speed than needed, the tip is pulled down and flexes back, which pulls the leader and fly back under the main line.

The main line is now well ahead of the leader and the fly as it is falling.

As all of the line falls to the water, the fly will continue to sink until all slack is removed from the leader.

The fly is well below the surface as the line begins drifting downstream.

Tuck Cast (Right Curve)

Start the forward cast with the rod tip angled to your left and the tip close to the water.

Continue to maintain this angle as the backcast unrolls.

Just before the line unrolls, begin the forward cast. During the forward cast keep the rod tip tilted. Generate a lot of line speed with a haul.

Speed up and stop on the forward cast just after the rod passes in front of you.

Aim the cast high. If you make a rapid speed-up-and-stop and hold the rod rock still after the stop, the tip flexes to the right. The front of the line, leader, and the fly curve to the right.

The front of the line, leader, and fly continue to fall in a curve to the right.

The fly line has curved to the right, and the slack will allow the weighted fly to sink quickly.

CURVE CASTS

A curve cast is just a tuck cast turned on its side, so many of the same principles that apply to the tuck apply to the curve. It works best with weighted flies and longish leaders, and the faster you bring the rod to a stop, and the heavier the weight on the leader, the more the line curves. You can throw a curve in the line pretty well with a dry fly, as long as the leader is short. There are two kinds of curve casts: sidearm and vertical. The easiest one to master is the sidearm curve, where you face the target and sweep the rod parallel to the water. The vertical curve is a challenging one but useful in some special situations.

> **The key to making any curve cast (sidearm or vertical) is that the rod tip must travel parallel to the water during the speed-up-and-stop.**

I learned the curve cast fishing for bonefish. Another great place for a curve cast is when you are fishing to laid-up tarpon, which on calm days or early in the morning suspend in the water with their dorsal or tail fins just sticking out of the water. If you throw a fly out in front of the fish and retrieve it, even a little 2-inch fly will spook a hundred-pound tarpon. But if you make a curve cast from behind the fish and then swim the fly across the front of the fish, you get a more natural presentation. One of the best flies for this, incidentally, is a Bucktail Deceiver. When it's dry, it lands like a feather, and unlike a sinking fly, it floats just under the surface film for some time, and you can pick it up quietly.

You don't want to attack fish with flies; you want to swim your fly away from the fish as if it was a fleeing baitfish. If the fish is looking away from the angler, a cast allows the fly to swim from one side across a fish's vision. If the fish is facing the angler, a curve cast allows the fly to be retrieved from one side to the other before making a turn toward the angler. Curve casts can be used to strategically lure the fish toward the fly but not toward the boat, which will spook it. Anytime you have a fish facing you—trout, bonefish, redfish, whatever—and you throw straight at the fish in the conventional manner, you draw the fish toward you, where it will eventually see the boat and spook. If you make a curve cast that swims the fly broadside to the fish, the fish will very often follow the fly, which is swimming away from it, and not see the boat.

I have since found many uses for this cast in fresh water. For trout, you can use a curve cast to swim a fly "along" a stream- or riverbank rather throwing the streamer at the bank and pulling it back toward them. The fish only sees the back end of the fly rather than its profile. Cast with a downstream curve tight to the bank, and you can strip your fly along the bank for a longer time. Bass often lie behind rocks and stumps. With a curve cast, you can cast a popper so that it hooks behind the rock or stump and begin your retrieve. Sometimes, you can't even see your fly, but rises are often audible and let you know when to set the hook.

Sidearm Curve to the Left

This is the easiest method of learning a curve cast. For a right-handed person, the curve will develop to the left. The

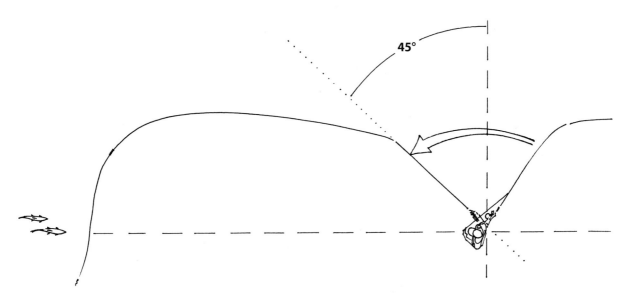

You must face the target for an accurate side curve cast. Make a low side backcast parallel to the water, and on the forward cast, stop the rod at a 45-degree angle from the target. The faster you stop the rod tip at 45 degrees, the more the tip curves inward, producing the side curve cast. If you always face the target and always stop the rod at 45 degrees from it, you will always throw the same cast. If you change the angle at which you face the target, then it becomes hard to ascertain the exact direction of the rod tip, and your curve casts are not as accurate.

key to making this cast is to face your target and have your rod tip travel parallel to the surface of the water, stopping your rod tip at 45 degrees to the target. The high-speed stop, coupled with the weight of the fly, flexes the rod tip to the left, and your line, leader, and fly all go in that direction. The faster (not harder) you move the rod tip during the speed-up-and-stop, the greater the curve.

To make accurate sidearm curve casts, it is important to face the target, and if that is north on a compass, you want to stop when the rod tip hits northeast, or 45 degrees to the target. By positioning your body so that you always face the target with this cast, and consistently stopping the rod tip at 45 degrees to the target, you can consistently make accurate curve casts at long distances.

Sidearm Curve to the Left

Begin with the rod low to the side and close to the water. Move the rod back to begin lifting line from the water. Make a low, climbing backcast. Just before the line unrolls, begin the forward cast.

Keep the rod at a lowered angle on the forward cast.

To develop accuracy, you need to make the same cast each time. Face the target. On the forward cast when the rod is at 45 degrees from the target, make an extra-fast speed-up-and-stop with the rod parallel to the water. The faster the rod tip speeds up and stops on the forward cast, the greater the curve will be. Hauling and accelerating faster will produce a larger curve in the line.

If the curve is to travel parallel to the surface, the rod tip during the speed-up-and-stop must travel parallel to the surface. Many have trouble with the curve because they start the forward cast with the rod too high and tend during the forward cast to bring the rod downward on the speed-up-and-stop. That will drive the fly downward (in the direction the tip stopped), resulting in little or no curve. What helps many people master this cast is to visualize the tip traveling slightly upward during the speed-up-and-stop.

After the speed-up-and-stop, slowly lower the rod tip.

The fly and leader curve to the left.

Vertical Curve to the Left

If you have structure on either side of you that prohibits making the side cast necessary to make a conventional curve cast, you can still make a curve cast in the vertical plane. The key to making any curve cast is that the tip must stay parallel to the water during the speed-up-and-stop—this is true for sidearm and vertical curve casts.

This is a difficult cast to master but worth the effort. When most people make this cast, they start with their hand up high,

so they come forward with their hand coming down. And as it comes down, if they speed up and stop with their wrists twisting to the left, unless the wrist stays parallel to the water, the tip doesn't stay parallel to the water, so they throw a cast that goes down and around, and the curve never has the opportunity to form.

Vertical Curve to the Left

Lower the rod for a backcast. When the line end leaves the water, make a vertical backcast and allow the line to unroll.

Just before the backcast unrolls completely, begin the forward cast.

Soon after the rod tip passes vertically in front of you, make a rapid speed-up-and-stop by twisting your wrist sharply inward. It is critical to make your wrist twist parallel to the surface. At the end of the speed-up-and-stop, your rod hand should be about center to the chest and your thumb pointing to the left and parallel to the water.

If you hold the rod high and twist your wrist parallel to the surface, you create a curve to the left. Your rod hand must travel in a tight, swift turn to the left to maintain the rod handle parallel with the water. If your rod hand descends on the speed-up-and-stop, there will be no curve. Keeping your hand parallel to the surface as it twists to the left causes the rod tip to twist sharply to the left, creating a shock wave to the left that will travel down the line. Note that the left curve is just starting to move away from the rod tip.

Keep the rod tip high while the line curves. Because the rod tip sped up and stopped parallel to the surface, the line is traveling parallel to the water. The curving shock wave created on the speed-up-and-stop is moving toward the line end. When learning this cast, anglers tend to twist the rod hand slightly downward and to the left, throwing the line in the water with no curve.

Don't be in a hurry to lower the rod tip. The shock wave travels through the leader and causes it and the fly to fall to the left. The faster the line travels and the more you twist your rod hand on the speed-up-and-stop, the greater the curve.

As the line end nears the target, begin to lower the rod tip.

Continue to lower the rod tip.

Before the fly touches down, the rod should be in a fishing position. The leader and fly have fallen in a large curve.

Vertical Curve to the Right

Right-handers can quickly learn to make an accurate curve to the left. But to cast a curve in the opposite direction is very difficult for most right-handers because they can't twist their wrists to the right—and they shouldn't try. Here is where an understanding of Principle 3 helps make a successful curve to the right. The line goes in the direction the tip speeds up and stops. To make a vertical cast to the right, the rod tip must travel parallel to the right on the speed-up-and-stop. Bring your forearm down until it's 45 degrees, and then you can turn your whole forearm and arm, concentrating on keeping the tip at the same height above the water while you do this.

Vertical Curve to the Right

Begin with the rod tip close to the surface, pointing in the direction of the target. If you are right-handed and want to make a curve to the right, you must tilt the rod across your body well to the left when drawing the line toward you. Make a backcast with the rod tilted slightly to the left of your shoulder. When you lift the end of the line from the water, make a backcast.

Allow the line to flow back.

As the backcast continues to unroll, tilt the rod farther to the side. Keep the rod high, with your elbow on the shelf and your thumb behind the rod handle away from the target. Begin the forward cast just before the backcast unrolls. Accelerate forward, keeping the rod tip high.

When the rod passes in front of you, make the right-hand curve. It is impossible to twist your wrist to make the curve, but the rod tip nonetheless needs to speed up and stop in a curving motion. To accomplish this, your forearm should be at 45 degrees (or slightly lower) in front of you. If the forearm is rotated during the speed-up-and-stop in a curving motion, the line will curve the same way.

As you rotate your forearm, the rod tip needs to stay at the same height, or parallel to the surface. If you angle the rod tip downward during the forearm's speed-up-and-stop, the line is directed downward. Here is where most anglers have a problem. If the forearm is at 45 degrees or slightly lower, the forearm, not the wrist, can curve to the right with the rod. It is vital that the rod hand stay parallel to the surface if the curve is to work. The fly will go in the direction the rod tip stops. You can monitor this by watching where your thumb and knuckles point. To make a curve that falls at a right angle to you, your thumb and knuckles stop pointing toward the desired spot.

This shows the leader and front portion of the line curving to the right. The rod stops with your knuckles and thumb pointing to the right.

After the speed-up-and-stop, you can begin lowering the rod.

Continue to lower the rod.

LOW-SIDE-UP CAST

Most fly rods are 8 to 9 feet long, and if you make an overhead cast, the line is traveling more than 10 feet above the surface. It's easy to alert fish in shallow or calm water, and with the overhead cast, if the unrolling line doesn't spook the fish, it most certainly will when it hits the water. The low-side-up cast keeps the fly line close to the surface and unseen. At the end of the cast, the leader and fly are directed upward. This expends all the energy and deposits the fly as if it parachuted down to the surface.

I first started using this cast for bonefish in the Florida Keys many years ago. The best fishing can be when the sun is high overhead, enabling you to see the fish. But this also makes it easier for fish to see you and the fly line. On a really calm day, problems compound because not only are the fish going to see the fly line with a conventional cast, but there is no chop on the water to mask the disturbance of the line and fly when they hit the water. If you cast with a normal overhead cast using a weighted bonefish fly, it is hard to get a relatively delicate presentation. For this reason, I include this cast under casts for weighted flies, but it also works really well with dry flies on a calm pool.

On calm pools in a trout stream, it's more often than not the line falling to the water that scares the fish. If you make a low-side-up cast, the fish is never going to see the line because it is going to be so low to the water, and the line is only going to fall a short distance to the water, which lessens the impact. Most important, in a vertical cast the end of the fly line often whips forward. In fact, a fly that is too heavy will often duck under and tangle from the force. With a proper low-side-up cast, the leader and the very forward portion of the line go up at the end of the cast, which exhausts all the cast's energy. So in effect, you get the same results as if you went out there and just released the fly a few feet above the water. You get a much softer presentation, you hardly get any noise from the fly hitting the water, and you keep the line out of the fish's sight. Because of the soft presentation, this cast might be a better choice than a regular sidearm cast, generally in very calm water—a big trout pool or laid-up tarpon in glassy water.

Low-Side-Up Cast

This is a stealth cast. Crouch if you are close to the fish. Point the rod at the fish and carefully draw the line back.

Continue drawing the line back low to the water.

When the line end leaves the water, make a low backcast.

The low-side-up cast is more difficult to make from a high rod angle, and you are more likely to alert the fish.

Just before the line unrolls, begin the forward cast.

In the beginning, the forward cast should be close to the surface.

As you accelerate the rod to just in front of your body, speed up and stop, going parallel to the surface but finishing upward. If made correctly, your thumb will point up on the stop. Study the photos above to understand how your rod hand must speed up and stop upward. If the cast ends with your thumb on the stop parallel to the water, a basic side cast results. The unrolling line comes forward close to the surface. Because the rod was kept low on the back and forward cast, the line is unseen by the fish.

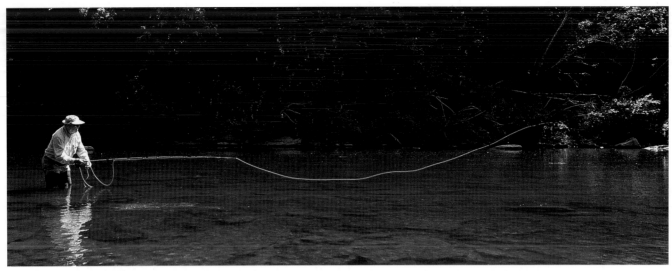

Most of the line is within a foot or two of the surface as it is falling, and the leader and fly have stopped going forward, exhausting the energy of the cast. Note the line is traveling low and unseen by the fish while the leader and fly are climbing.

The line has gently dropped to the surface, and the line end and the fly are settling softly to the water.

As the cast ends, you are in a position to begin fishing.

CASTING WEIGHTED LINES

Fly fishermen often complain about casting weighted lines, which can be a sinking tip, sinking head, or complete sinking line, and weighted flies. They have so much trouble casting weight that they often refuse to use it, limiting their pleasure and what they can catch. Weighted line and flies will let anglers reach fish that would otherwise never see their offerings.

When saltwater fly fishing, I would rather cast a lead-core shooting head than a floating line—there is so little effort required. Because of their thin diameter and weight, weighted lines load the rod better, cast heavier or more air-resistant flies, go a longer distance, and can be thrown more easily on windy days. When casting a floating line and a fly of little weight, the line begins to slow near the end of the cast. The opposite occurs with weighted lines and flies. Once the weighted line or flies are set in motion, they tend to continue in that direction. It is the abrupt change in direction from the back to forward cast that causes so many fly casters trouble with weighted lines and flies. When a trout fisherman is casting a long leader with a fly on the end, a dropper, a split shot, and an indicator, the abrupt change in direction from back to forward cast is why the leader tangles badly. Learning to make a smooth transition from back to forward cast avoids those tangles.

The other huge problem with these types of rigs is hitting yourself or hitting your rod with them. Once you get two-thirds of the way around the horseshoe, if your hand is behind your body, you can then elevate the cast so that it travels high above your head: You avoid hitting yourself and you avoid hitting your rod, which can be disastrous if you hit your rod with a heavily weighted fly. On the forward cast, once the hand gets even with the body, then the backcast is being directed at you or your rod tip. Begin the forward cast farther behind you to prevent hitting yourself. If you cast low and sidearm, you can start the forward cast behind your body, which keeps everything away from your head.

When casting sinking lines, a lot of anglers have trouble with the end of the line dumping at the end of the cast. If they make a straight cast, the line dumps under in a pile, but, even worse, if they twist their wrists at all, the line dumps and curves to the left or the right (think unintentional curve cast here) and ruins their accuracy. The rod should come forward vertically—over the top—for the most accurate cast. That should prevent any curving to one side or the other. To prevent any dumping, don't make the forward cast too fast. The backcast is what loads the rod; when you make the forward cast, just come through smoothly and gently. Also, you might try lengthening the leader a little bit. The leader acts like a tail on a kite and helps turn the line over better. The same thing applies when you are using floating lines with steep, heavy front tapers, such as saltwater or bass lines.

I am first going to show two useful casts for floating lines, the basic water haul and the Belgian cast, and then more specialized casts and techniques building on the basic skills you'll learn in these casts.

Basic Water Haul with Floating Line

This lob cast is the best way that I know of to easily cast tangle-free weighted flies and leaders with split shot and indicators on them. I often recommend that beginners use this cast to become comfortable casting multiple flies or nymphs with shot before moving on to the next cast, the weighted line cast, also called the Belgian, or oval, cast. Weighted nymphs create casting problems because of the quick change in direction from back to forward cast. Anyone who fished minnows or hellgrammites on a fly rod years ago like I did soon discovered that a quick change of direction during casting meant a loss of the bait. The water haul allows you to change directions smoothly and eliminate problems like hitting yourself or your rod with the weighted fly or flies or tangling the leader. This sequence shows how to smoothly lift two weighted flies and make a smooth forward cast.

Basic Water Haul with Floating Line

Two weighted nymphs have been fished through productive water and need to be recast for another drift. Because the nymphs are weighted, a conventional cast with a quick change of direction can cause problems. Lower the rod to remove slack.

Start the backcast with your thumb behind the target and do not twist your wrist. Cast a wide, slow loop to prevent tangles and follow through with the rod tip.

As soon as the backcast ends, lower the rod tip almost to the water, extend your arm to the rear, and shift your body weight back.

As soon as the fly touches down (don't let it sink), begin drawing the rod forward.

Don't rush the cast and smoothly draw the rod forward. It will begin to load. There has been no abrupt change in direction.

Continue to smoothly move the rod forward. This will lift the line and fly from the water and load the rod.

The two weighted flies are smoothly rising from the water as you begin the forward cast.

Aim the cast rather high so that the weighted flies will travel well above you.

As soon as the flies have passed in front of you, begin to lower the rod.

The water haul allows you to cast multiple flies (or leader with split shot) easy without tangles.

Casting Weighted Flies with Floating Line

This cast uses the same motions as with a sinking line, but you don't need to roll cast to get the line to the surface of the water because you are fishing with a floating line that doesn't sink. This cast is useful for fishing multiple fly rigs, nymphs with indicators and split shot, or heavy flies such as Clouser Deep Minnows on floating lines.

Once weighted flies (or weighted lines, such as a shooting heads, sinking tip lines, lead-core shooting heads) are in motion, they want to continue in motion. Unweighted flies and floating lines tend to slow near the end of the backcast, but not so with weighted flies or lines. If you false-cast weighted flies and your timing is not perfect, all sorts of problems arise. By adjusting your backcast, you should not have to false cast.

Casting Weighted Flies with Floating Line

Start with the rod tip low and pointing toward the fly.

To make an easy and comfortable cast with a sinking line or fly, make a low side backcast. Try to keep the tip close to the surface on the backcast. If you take the rod back too high on the forward cast, you could hit yourself or your rod with the fly.

If you make a conventional vertical cast, the sinking line or weighted fly will travel rearward at great speed. When the forward cast begins, the abrupt change in direction produces shock waves and makes for a difficult forward cast. To avoid an abrupt change of direction, after the rod has passed behind you, make a circular speed-up-and-stop to create a wide, rounded backcast loop.

When you rotate the rod tip around in a circle, don't twist your wrist; instead rotate your forearm while keeping your elbow on the imaginary shelf. It might help you to imagine the rod tip is inside a horseshoe turned on its side.

Let the loop unroll while keeping your arm in motion, bringing it around in a half circle. It is important to keep your elbow on the shelf and your rod hand low as the forward cast begins. The motion between the back and forward casts is continuous.

Well before the wide loop unrolls, begin the forward cast to ensure a smooth transition from the backcast to the forward cast.

The cast should be a climbing one.

Begin the speed-up-and-stop when the rod is about vertical. Cast a wider loop. Tight loops may tangle the leader or fly.

If the line and fly travel well overhead, you won't hit yourself. When making a longer cast, aim the forward cast so that it is climbing, and it will travel farther before gravity sets in.

Lower the rod as the loop finishes unrolling.

Continue to lower the rod so that you are in a fishing position before the fly touches the water.

Water Haul with Sinking Line

During the retrieve, a weighted fly or sinking line swims well down in the water column. You must roll cast the line and fly to the surface to make an easy backcast. Once the weighted line or fly is on the surface, water tension pulls against the line on the water, helping you to deepen the load in the rod. In the sequence shown here, I am casting a weighted shooting head.

Before making a backcast, roll cast the weighted fly line to the surface. Remove all slack from the line and lower the rod tip.

Raise the rod to lift the line until the end is free of the water. Keep your elbow on the shelf.

Retrieve enough line so that you can lift all the line from the surface.

Once the line is out of the water, continue to bring the rod back, dragging the leader and fly to the surface.

With the rod well behind and all the line, leader, and fly on the surface, you can make a roll cast.

Carry your rod hand straight forward, lifting the line and fly from the water, and speed up and stop. A single haul often helps.

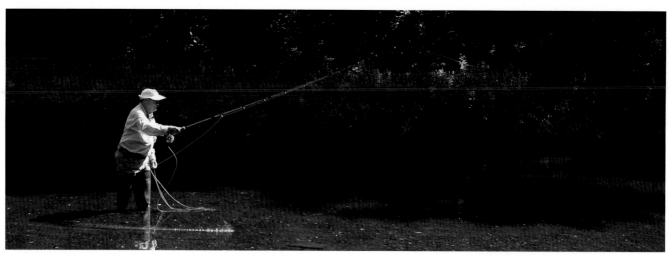

This roll cast should unroll the line and lay it out straight in the surface. If it doesn't, try again rather than picking up for a backcast. Avoid false casting—it takes years to learn to false cast weighted lines.

As soon as the speed-up-and-stop directs the line and fly straight ahead, lower the rod to the surface. Note that I have shot a little bit of the running line through the guides, and there is a proper amount of overhang when I begin the backcast.

When the sinking line or fly touches down after the roll cast, begin drawing the rod back low and to the side. Don't wait too long or the line or fly will sink below the surface, and it will be difficult to make the backcast. A single haul helps.

The lower the rod is drawn back, the easier it is to make the proper forward cast.

The moment the fly leaves the water, make a continuous, rounded speed-up-and-stop. A normal, straight speed-up-and-stop will cause an abrupt change of direction from the back to forward cast, creating shock waves in the line. Instead, the line and fly should travel around a curve on the backcast. The faster the line travels around the circular path on the backcast, the more line speed is generated and the deeper the rod is loaded. To increase the line speed and rod loading, a fast, continuous single haul while the rod is accelerating will produce a longer cast, aiding in throwing heavier lines and flies. If enough speed is generated on the circular backcast, little effort is required to make a long and efficient forward cast.

Keep moving the rod in a continuous circular motion during the backcast.

Make the forward cast at a towering angle.

Speed up and stop upward while the rod hand is still slightly behind your body. This causes the fly to travel well above you and also prevents the fly from striking the rod tip.

This is one of the few casts where your elbow should be well above the shelf at the end of the cast.

Because of the climbing angle of your forward cast, the line and fly pass well above your head. There is no need to "chuck and duck" on the forward cast. Shoot line through the guides as soon as you stop the rod. This method requires only one circular backcast when performed correctly.

To obtain maximum distance on a cast, release the running line.

All line has been shot to the target. If accuracy is more important than distance, shoot the line through an O in your fingers, trapping the line when the fly is over the target. You know that you have made a good cast when all the remaining line shoots through the guides and pulls tight.

Double Water Haul with Sinking Line

I learned this cast years ago from Californian Harry Kime, who has caught thousands of giant tarpon, probably more than any other fly fisherman. Kime used to stay several months a year and fish daily at Casa Mar, a tarpon camp on the northeast coast of Costa Rica. When he was in his 80s, Kime found because of his diminishing strength that he needed to modify his casting to make his presentation easier, and he developed the double water haul. With it, he could cast a 30-foot shooting head and a giant Whistler all day.

This cast is for when you really want to do things easily with sinking lines. After roll casting your line to the surface, flop it back onto the water behind you in a more vertical plane and let the line fall behind you on the water, with your arm outstretched, rod tip low to the water. The rod and line should be in a long, straight line. As soon as the front end of the line (near the leader) contacts the water, begin to draw on the line, and then before your hand reaches your body, make a forward cast at an elevated angle and slowly bring it forward, loading the rod. The cast will go twice as far as it would if you cast it the regular way because the rod is loaded by pulling against the water. I also use this cast when nymph fishing and using multiple flies and split shot, and when fishing out of a boat. A lot of false casting tends to make the guy rowing the boat a little nervous. Also, because you are coming back more vertically instead of sidearm, the cast takes up less space, which is good in a boat.

The example here demonstrates how to get extra distance with a heavy shooting head. But the double water haul can be used with shorter casts—for example, when changing directions while fishing heavy streamers and nymphs. While it was developed for sinking lines, you can also use floating lines with this cast.

Double Water Haul with Sinking Line

After retrieving a heavy sinking shooting head, make a single water haul.

Draw the rod back to lift the line. With a small amount of overhang, raise the rod to get as much of the sinking line as possible near the surface.

Continue to lift the line with the rod. If too much line is left underwater before the backcast, you will not be able to lift all line from the water.

Drop the rod back to drag the line and fly on the surface.

Make a roll cast, directing the line straight ahead.

As soon as the fly is delivered straight ahead, lower the rod near the surface. It is important to begin a water haul with the rod low.

Begin a single water haul.

Your thumb should be behind the handle away from the target, and during the backcast do not twist your wrist while you haul the line against the surface tension.

When the end of the line leaves the water, speed up and stop, simultaneously making a single haul. If you have kept your thumb behind the handle, the line will travel in a straight line behind you.

After you speed up and stop, lower the rod tip while the fly is in flight.

The moment the fly and front of the line touch the water behind you, begin a long drawing motion with the rod while hauling to begin the forward cast. The surface tension gripping the line bends and loads the rod deeply.

A climbing angle of flight is desirable for the line and fly, so your elbow begins to rise from the shelf as your rod hand comes forward.

Speed up and stop immediately after the line end leaves the water and while your rod hand is slightly behind your body. The angle of flight is determined by the angle of the speed-up-and-stop.

The heavy line (and possibly the attached fly) should travel well above you so it doesn't strike you or the rod. To accomplish this, direct the cast upward and speed up and stop earlier than with a normal forward cast.

The angle of flight is roughly 45 degrees, causing the line and fly to travel well above you.

Just before the line unrolls, lower the rod to a fishing position. Keep your arm and rod elevated as all the running line shoots through the guides.

Overhang

A shooting taper (more commonly called a shooting head) has two parts: The forward portion or head can be a floating line, a fast sinking line, or anything in between. The rear portion (commonly referred to as the shooting line) is a much thinner and lighter line. These lines could be separate and connected with a loop-to-loop connection, or they can be integrated into one fly line. Because the thinner shooting line offers so little resistance when going through the guides, the heavier head can travel great distances. When you're fishing with sinking heads, greater depths can be obtained with the fly because the shooting line offers less resistance to the water than a conventional fly line.

When you're casting, the amount of shooting line outside the rod tip is called overhang. Too little running line outside the rod tip limits distance. Too much running line outside the tip won't support the heavier head as it turns over to unroll toward the target. The ideal amount of overhang differs with each rod/line combination and angler. A fly fisherman with three rod and line combinations will determine that a different overhang length may be necessary with the individual outfits. To determine the correct overhang is easy. Too much overhang, and you'll see shock waves in the line. Too little overhang, and you don't get maximum distance. When getting used to a new line, false cast it, adding a little more shooting line each false cast. When small shock waves appear, retract enough of the shooting line until the waves disappear.

Jim Green, designer of many Fenwick rods and the modern ferrule system on most fly rods, was a great tournament caster and the one who introduced me to shooting heads. In the sixties Jim used to come to Florida to fish with me, and he taught me about overhang, and that false casting shooting heads was a lot more difficult than using a water haul to send your line on its way after one backcast. Jim was also the one who taught me to make that forward cast with your hand behind your body so that you could throw upward and avoid hitting yourself or your rod with a weighted fly.

I don't know why this is, and perhaps someone can explain the physics to me sometime, but if you shoot a little extra line on your backcast (before the final presentation cast) and extend your overhang, you do not cause shock waves in the line and you can cast much farther. You effectively increase the amount of overhang for your forward cast—more than I would recommend picking up—but it doesn't cause shock waves.

> *Begin casting with no overhang, and gradually work out more running line until you start to get shock waves, to see the limits of your tackle. Too much overhang causes shock waves and other problems; too little overhang and you won't get maximum distance.*

Too Much Overhang

The orange line is the running line and the white line is the shooting head. About 7 feet of running line is outside the rod tip as you raise the rod to lift line from the water. This is too much overhang for most casters.

After you begin the forward cast, the line at the rod tip must begin unrolling, pulling the rest of the line forward. The shooting line is so thin that it collapses under the weight of the heavy head. You have too much overhang when you see shock waves in the line as it unrolls forward of the tip.

These shock waves undulate through the fly line.

Shock waves create tangles in the line, tailing loops, and poor presentations.

Proper Overhang

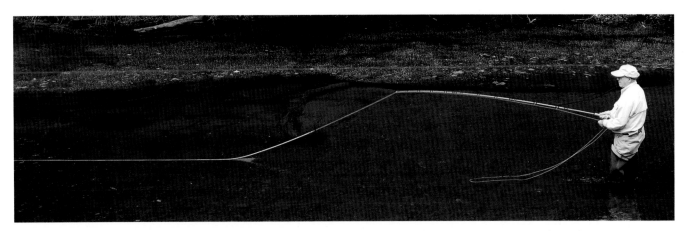

For most anglers 1 to 3 feet is the best amount of overhang. Advanced casters can handle more. Lower the rod and remove all slack from the line before lifting the line from the water.

Begin the forward cast just before the backcast unrolls. Hauling shortens the length of the overhang.

The rod accelerates forward. Only a short amount of overhang is outside the tip, and the loop is smooth. Gradually work out more overhang until you see shock waves, shorten the overhang until they disappear, and that is the right amount of overhang for you and your rod and line.

As the loop unrolls, lower the rod.

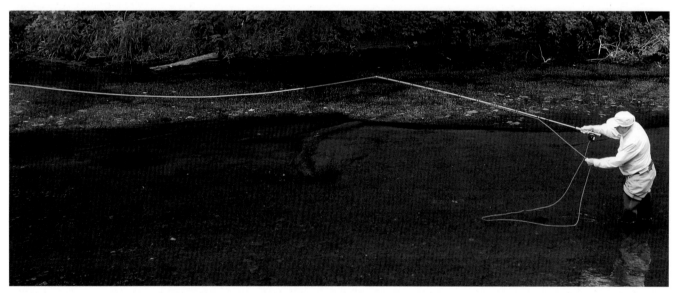

The line has no shock waves in it as the forward cast travels to the target.

CHAPTER 12

Managing Line

With conventional and spinning tackle, the reel stores the line until it is cast. Fly fishermen have to learn how to control or manage the loose line lying on the deck or in the water. There are devices and casts that do this.

STRETCHING LINE

When you pull many fly lines from the reel, they retain the position in which they were stored on the reel—in tight coils. Stretch the line to remove these coils to improve your casting.

Stretching Line

This line has been pulled from the spool and is in tight coils.

Slip the line under your foot. Grasp the line on both sides about shoulder high and pull firmly with both hands, but not excessively hard. This method can be used in a boat or along the stream and doesn't harm the line as long as your shoe soles are clean and you use only enough force to stretch out the coils.

The coils have been removed between the hands. Continue the process until you have removed all the coils.

SHOOTING LINE

At the end of a forward cast, it is important to retain line control. You may be casting to a cruising fish that takes the fly as soon as it hits the water. If you are looking for the line to begin stripping, you may miss your opportunity to strike. Sometimes you realize that your forward cast is going wrong, and you can trap the line and make another false cast. You can also trap the line for accuracy. An experienced spinning or plug fisherman makes a cast that would deliver the lure or bait well beyond the target. But to obtain accuracy as the lure or bait nears the target, the cast is slowed by a spin fisherman by feathering the line or the plug caster by applying pressure to the revolving spool, and they stop the cast when the lure or bait is over the target. The average fly fisherman makes a cast and hopes to God the fly lands near the target. If you are blind casting, then letting go of the line on the forward cast is okay. Otherwise, retain control.

Uncontrolled Shooting Line

I haul on the forward cast.

Without control of the line, it often wraps several times over the rod, which can snag the line on the stripping guide and ruin the cast.

As the line begins shooting through the rod guides, I let go of the fly line. There is no chance to control the accuracy of the cast.

Controlled Shooting Line

Begin your forward cast.

Form an O ring with the thumb and first finger, allowing the line to shoot through it.

Speed up and stop the rod at a slight climbing angle. This angle allows you to stop the unrolling cast anytime you wish.

Gradually lower the rod as the line flows through your fingers.

During the entire forward cast, concentrate on the target.

When almost all of the line has been shot, move the finger controlling the line close to the reel.

Making an O with your fingers prevents the line from wrapping around the stripping guide on a high-speed cast.

As the cast ends, transfer the line in the left hand to the rod hand.

Most of the line has been shot to the target. You can trap the line at any time to drop it accurately on the target.

As the fly lands, you are now ready to begin your retrieve or set the hook if a fish strikes immediately.

STRIPPING AND SHOOTING COILS

When you are wading deep and need to cast a long line, it's easy to get a messy tangle or lose distance because of the line tension on the water. If you control the coils of line as you retrieve the fly, you can usually shoot it trouble-free.

There are other ways to accomplish controlling loose lines, but I have found this one offers several advantages over some. This method reduces the amount of line lying on the water, making it easier to shoot line better. If properly stored, the line rarely tangles on the shoot. And it permits the angler to move to another position with the coils of loose line under control. Some people like to place coils in their clenched lips. But I don't recommend this method because of *Giardia* and the questionable water quality on many of the rivers we fish.

Stripping and Shooting Coils

Grip the line with your line hand as you would in a normal retrieve. Retrieve about 10 feet of line, allowing it to fall on the water beside you.

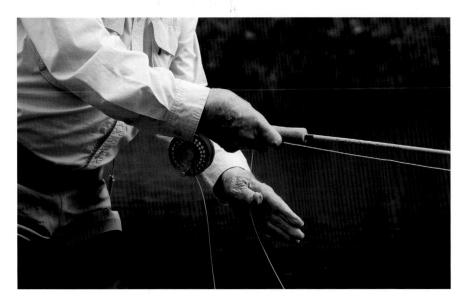

Before retrieving more line, position it at the joint of your thumb and hand and hold it firmly there.

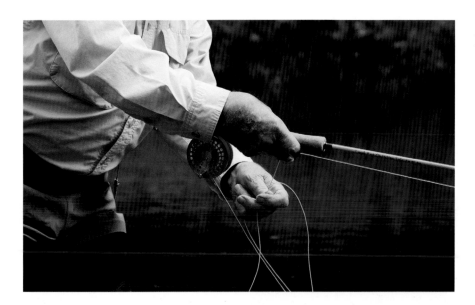

Retrieve about another 10 feet of line.

Place the line under the thumb and finger about an inch or so forward of the line you trapped earlier.

You should now have two big loops. Retrieve the final 10 feet of line.

Trap the line now under the forward end of the thumb.

You are now ready to make the backcast. Keep the three loops apart by your fingers.

Make the backcast while firmly holding the three loops of line.

Make a regular backcast, preparing to let go of one of the coils when you make a forward cast.

Begin coming forward, accelerating and loading the rod while hauling.

Speed up and stop, forming a loop.

Shoot one of the coils on the forward cast.

As the coil continues to shoot out . . .

. . . trap the line and begin hauling for a backcast.

Begin the backcast, and at the same time begin hauling.

Accelerate the rod back.

End your haul as you speed up and stop on the backcast, shooting the second coil.

Shooting the second coil.

Begin moving your line hand toward your rod hand to haul before the final presentation cast.

Accelerate the rod forward, hauling.

Keep accelerating forward to load the rod deeply.

Shoot the last coil and the remaining line after you stop the rod.

Sometimes extending your arm at the end helps the line shoot through the guides.

The line tension on the water helps the coils shoot without tangling.

The line continues to travel to the target.

To shoot a lot of line, you need to generate a lot of line speed with a good haul. The line was traveling so fast through the guides on this cast that I could have shot an extra 10 or 15 feet if I would have had it coiled up.

Note: When making this cast, you can shoot all three coils with only one backcast by shooting all the line that you hold. But it is easier to learn if you make two backcasts.

STRIPPING BASKETS

Stripping baskets are simply containers attached to the body into which you deposit retrieved line. Some baskets are meant to be worn in front, others at the side, and most can be repositioned depending on what is comfortable for you. I have always been more comfortable with a side stripping basket, but this is simply a matter of choice. Most stripping baskets are held in place by a belt or elastic strap or band. I prefer a shoulder strap for a side basket and an adjustable strap that

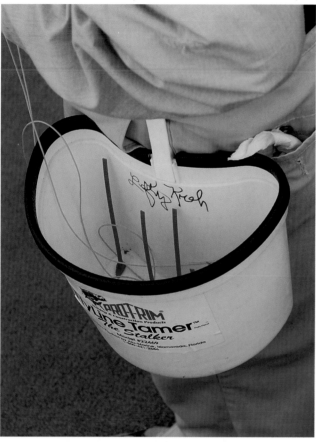

Cable ties in my Stalker basket hold the line in place when I am moving about but allow the line to flow freely on the cast.

also secures it to the leg so that the basket stays in position, even if you have to run down the beach after breaking fish.

A stripping basket is useful for all kinds of fly fishing. Surf fishermen are plagued with line dropping into the suds and becoming a tangled mess. Many fish have eluded anglers in boats who somehow stood on the line, or it caught on something in the boat, ruining the cast. Even trout fishermen who move along a stream dragging line behind them or having it snag in the grass can profit by it. Any trout fisherman who has cast from the back of a drift boat knows how many things can catch the line. In addition to preventing snags, baskets keep line cleaner by preventing it from getting underfoot on a dirty deck or, even worse, on a sandy beach.

There are several stripping basket designs, ranging from buckets (VLMD, vertical line management devices) that sit on the boat deck to baskets that you wear. There are even flat mats with "fingers" that hold the line dropped to the deck at the angler's feet. Some of the best designs are baskets that collapse or fold so they can be placed in a duffle bag and accompany the fly fisherman on a distant trip. I predict that more and more fly fishermen will see the value of these baskets and use them. All have a use, and you have the option of buying one manufactured for fly fishers or building your own. When wading while fishing the flats for bonefish or permit and especially when freshwater trout fishing, you may only need a relatively short line, and a large stripping basket is unnecessary. A basket also comes in handy to prevent grass from snagging your line when stalking trout along a weedy bank or when hiking from pool to pool. The basket that I like is called The Stalker, and for information concerning it, contact Alu-Marine Corp., P.O. Box 1332, Islamorada, FL 33036.

Because baskets can get water in them from waves or when wading deep, I prefer many relatively large drain holes in a side basket. And *all* stripping baskets should have cones or other "fingers" to hold the retrieved line in place. In homemade baskets, many prefer to use cable ties for these fingers.

Side Stripping Basket

Many anglers feel that they can retrieve line more comfortably with a side basket. It is advisable, as with a VLMD, that you put in the basket a little more line than is cast. That way, at the beginning of each retrieve, the line in the basket helps bring the retrieved line in, too. If you cast all the line each time, you then have to place the first part of the rear line in the basket. If you have some line remaining in the basket when the cast finishes, it helps feed the line into the basket better.

Just before the line unrolls, make a forward cast.

When you stop the rod, the line begins to shoot from the basket.

When the retrieve ends, make a backcast.

The line flows freely without tangles.

All the line has been shot from the basket—tangle-free.

Front Stripping Basket

Once you have retrieved the line into the stripping basket, begin a new forward cast.

On the forward cast, the line flows smoothly from the basket and through the controlling hand.

Come forward and speed up and stop.

Even though the line is traveling fast, it comes from the basket tangle-free.

The forward cast ends.

Use a hand-over-hand retrieve, making sure to drop all line into the basket.

The retrieve begins. The rod is pointed at the fly.

Continue the hand-over-hand retrieve until you are ready to pick up line for the backcast.

VLMD (Vertical Line Management Device)

The VLMD is most useful when fishing from a boat. It does limit somewhat where and how you can move when casting, but it has many advantages. The height of the VLMD is critical. I like one where the upper edge is about even with my crotch. The first VLMD was the Line Tamer developed by Karl Anderson, who lives in the Florida Keys. Other models are available. Many fly fishermen prefer to place a little water in the bottom, believing that it allows the line to shoot with fewer tangles. Some VLMDs also have upright "fingers" in the bottom to hold the line in position as it is retrieved, reducing tangles on the cast.

For best results, add a little more line to the VLMD than you will cast. This permits the line to better fall into the VLMD as each retrieve begins. I prefer to keep the VLMD between my two legs so that when retrieving I always know exactly where to drop line. If I change position, I simply pick up the VLMD and move it so it is between my legs in the new casting direction.

When moving from one location to another, the line need not be spooled back on the reel but can remain in the VLMD. Upon arriving at the next location, simply pick up the rod and start casting. These buckets improve your casts so much, some anglers take them with them on trips to ensure they have them even if their guides don't. If you have fished out of boats in other countries, the VLMD is a real blessing. Dan Blanton, others, and myself store our gear and clothes for a trip in a VLMD and then place it in a bag with wheels and check it at the airport. Some very light, folding VLMDs can be carried in a duffle bag, and some anglers use the collapsible lawn and leaf buckets available in many home improvement stores.

Line Tamer

With the VLMD between my legs, I have just finished a retrieve.

A backcast begins.

The forward cast begins. The line shoots out of the VLMD.

All of the line is shot to the target without tangles. Note that some of the line remains in the VLMD, assuring that during the retrieve the line begins falling into the container.

Line continues to flow freely out of the VLMD.

SPEED CASTS

Anglers discovered in the 1960s when learning to fish for tarpon and bonefish that you often couldn't stand there and take 10 minutes to work out as much line as you need to cast to the fish. You were at the mercy of the fish. You'd be poling along when all of a sudden a bonefish would show up and you had to do something. You couldn't have all that line stripped out ahead of time and dragging around in the water—it would get tangled up in the grass—and you couldn't have it on the boat deck where it would get blown around. You had to learn to make speed casts, where you hold the fly in one or the other hand, to get the fly to a fish with as few false casts as possible. The basic speed cast is the easiest to learn, but your range is limited. The second sequence, the longer version of the speed cast, is good for distances of 40 to 60 feet.

Speed Cast

This is the safest method of holding the fly and line ready for a quick cast. Extend about 10 feet of line outside the rod tip. Hold the line just behind the first stripping guide. The rod hand holds the rod and the fly. The thumb and finger hold the hook so the point is free and points away from you and you won't be impaled.

Lower the rod tip almost to the water in the direction of the fish.

Begin the backcast. The lower the rod, the more it can be loaded. Many people do not lower the rod enough and have difficulty getting a fast backcast.

It is important to clench the fly just firmly enough that the resistance helps load the rod but lightly enough so that late in the backcast the rod pulls the fly from your fingers. Release the fly too early in the stroke, and the rod has nothing to pull against and doesn't load well.

A short, fast haul helps speed the line to the rear.

Try to get the rod well behind you so that a longer forward stroke is possible.

Just before the line unrolls on the backcast, begin sweeping the rod forward.

Haul while you accelerate the rod forward. Shoot line through your hand, but do not let it go. You will only have to recapture it after the fly hits the target. This may cause you to look for the line and lose sight of the fish.

Longer Speed Cast

This is a more difficult speed cast to master, but allows you to cast almost twice the amount of line of the conventional speed cast. Too often a fish appears close to a flats boat, and the basic speed cast allows a single forward cast of only about 12 feet of line and leader. The longer speed cast adds another 10 or 12 feet to the first forward cast—often the difference between hooking a fish or not. It also allows you to cast farther quicker because you are loading the original forward cast with more line outside the guides.

Longer Speed Cast

Hold the rod as shown here with the line running under your second finger and with about 15 to 18 feet of line and leader extended outside the rod tip.

Hold the fly in your line hand, and when you make the backcast, reach back and grab the fly line to gain control of the cast. If the line is under your second finger, a gap forms during the backcast so that you can slip your hand inside that loop and grasp the fly line.

If you trap the line against the rod with your finger, it is hard to grasp the line.

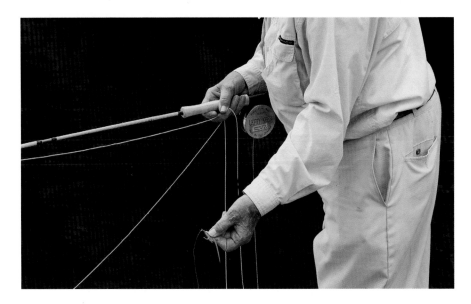

Hold the fly so the hook point won't impale your fingers on the cast.

Drape the front of the line over your finger about 4 to 5 feet from the nail knot. Do not curl your largest finger. During the backcast, the line will slip freely into the air. If you curl your finger around the line, it often spoils the backcast. It is now possible to hold all of the line, leader, and fly in a ready-to-cast position without any line dragging overboard.

When you spot a fish and are ready to cast, lower the rod tip close to the water toward the fish.

Clench the hook firmly with your finger and thumb as you rapidly sweep the rod up and back opposite the fish.

Holding the hook causes the rod to bend and load before it pulls the fly free on the backcast.

With practice, you can reach up and grasp the line as it travels back. But when first learning the cast, make a backcast, a forward cast, and during the second backcast, grasp the line. This shows the hand reaching up to grasp the line. Once you grasp the line, begin the forward cast, hauling during rod's acceleration.

Again, here is a view of how you should be holding the rod so that you can easily grab the line.

Grab the line behind you and begin the forward cast and your haul.

Begin the forward cast and the haul.

Accelerating the rod and hauling with the extra long line outside the rod tip allow the rod to load deeply, which enables you to develop high line speed and a tight loop. On the speed-up-and-stop, shoot the line toward the target by allowing it to flow through your hand. The line is under complete control, and you can stop the fly accurately. You also never have to take your eyes off your target. As the cast ends, place the line under your stripping finger to begin the retrieve.

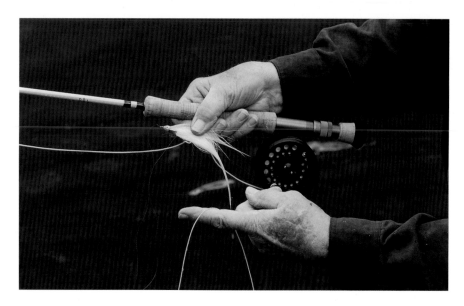

Susquehanna River guide Mike O'Brien showed me a version of this speed cast that he teaches to his clients. Follow the same instructions as for the speed cast but start by holding the fly in the rod hand. Experiment to find what works best for you.

Longer Speed Cast with Extra Backcast

There are times while standing on the bow of the boat that you need to make a longer than normal cast quickly. The speed cast with an extra false cast allows you to swiftly deliver a fly as far as 60 feet, if needed, while holding just the leader and line for a normal speed cast.

Longer Speed Cast with Extra Backcast

Trap the line just in front of the reel with your second finger (see close-ups of speed cast). Hold the fly between your thumb and first finger with the hook pointed toward the fish. About 15 feet of line is outside the rod tip. Drape the line about 3 feet before the leader butt over your middle finger. When you spot the fish, lower the rod tip and point it at the fish to permit the longest possible stroke to accelerate the line and load the rod.

Sweep the rod directly away from the fish. Clenching the fly between your thumb and finger so that the rod must pull it free helps load the rod. If you throw the fly into the air, the rod has nothing to pull against and doesn't load deeply.

As the line and fly sweep back, raise your line hand.

Continue to raise your hand toward the line trapped just in front of your second finger until it can grasp the line. When first learning this, do not attempt to grasp the line on the first backcast. Instead, make a forward cast and then grab the line. But with practice, learning to grasp the line as the rod travels rearward on the first backcast makes a much faster presentation.

Haul as the forward cast begins so that you can shoot extra line.

Just before the line completely unrolls, make a backcast.

Hauling helps load the rod and gives the line extra speed.

You shoot more line on the backcast.

The line straightens behind you.

Accelerating the rod and hauling on the forward cast is possible with a lot more line in the air than at the beginning. More line unrolls toward the fish while you control the cast by allowing the line to flow through the O ring formed with the thumb and first finger. This allows the line to be trapped accurately during the cast. As the fly drops to the water, you are ready to retrieve, and you have watched the fish during the entire cast.

CHAPTER 13

Going for Distance

In most freshwater situations, anglers who can cast to 45 or 50 feet can handle just about any casting chore that confronts them. Trout fishermen generally cast no more than 50 feet. Things are different when you go for steelhead in salt water or Atlantic salmon on big rivers. The ability to throw a longer line becomes vital to success. This is not to say that you shouldn't try to get close to fish if possible, but many times that just isn't possible.

There are a hundred situations where having an extra 20 or 30 feet cast can make all the difference in the world. Sometimes you can't move closer to the fish, whether you are limited because of water depth or other conditions, or you don't have enough time to get closer. In many freshwater situations, the angler can move around, get into position, and then cast. In salt water frequently you have to make a quick cast from where you are, and it may not be the best position. Or the wind may be blowing so hard that you need to cast 80 feet to get 35. Unfortunately, nature doesn't let saltwater fly fishermen cast downwind very often. Saltwater, lakes, and big rivers have few wind-free days. Another common situation where you need to make a longer cast is when you are blind fishing. A long retrieve is often many times more productive than a short one. When you are working open water, the longer you can swim the fly, the more likely you are to put it in front of a fish.

Many anglers (who generally can't cast very far) counter that you can't hook fish at long distances. This is true for giant tarpon and billfish that have hard mouths, but almost all other species can be hooked at great distances if you hold the rod low during the retrieve and the hooks are sharp. If you

> **For a long cast, the rod tip should be below your head when the rod tip passes beyond your body.**

cannot consistently cast beyond 50 feet, I urge you to try to improve your distance. It's true that you can catch a lot of fish closer than 50 feet, but it is no shame to be able to effortlessly throw a long line.

ELEMENTS OF DISTANCE CASTING

Anyone with skill can throw up to 80 or 90 feet with most lines. Beyond that distance, you need strength to sweep a rod through a long stroke at an ever-increasing speed and then bring it to an abrupt stop. Only strong people can accelerate the rod incredibly fast and then stop the tip dead to deliver all the energy toward the target. Many young or strong anglers can throw incredibly long distances (but in my view inefficiently) because they have the strength for the incredibly rapid stroke and are able to stop the rod abruptly. Were they efficient casters, they could increase their distance even more.

Tackle

Modern fly rods are moderate or fast action. I haven't seen what I regard as a slow-action rod in the past decade. A moderate-action rod will bend farther down from the tip than a fast-action rod under equal tension. For good casters, a fast-action rod can store more energy and stop quicker—simply because it is a bit stiffer. However, for most fly fishermen, stiffer rods require a greater sense of timing when casting.

Rods rated for lines from size 1 to 6 are generally designed for presentation and will be slower, allowing the fly to be presented to the fish quietly, and they are almost always used by freshwater trout fishermen. Rods rated for 8- to 10-weight lines are designed for transportation and will cast a fly a long distance. Often, delicate presentations are not a consideration. Rods rated for 12-weight and higher may cast moderately well at relatively short distances but are designed for fighting giant tarpon and offshore species that once brought to boat side must be lifted to be caught or to be released. The 7- to 11-weight rods are like the 16-gauge shotgun—a little too much for some situations, and not enough for others.

The size of the stripping guide on the butt section can affect casting distance. When shooting line, the line is traveling at a high speed, undulating, and does not slide through the guide easily. By using a larger guide (just as we do with spinning rods), the line is less constricted and flows more easily through to the target. Manufacturers have to sell you what you want to buy, and many anglers will not purchase a rod with an extra-large butt guide. I would suggest that all rods 8 through 10 have a butt guide no less than 20 mm, and a slightly larger guide is even better. If you don't know how to replace your smaller guide, any competent fly shop can do this for you.

Fly lines can also influence how far you can cast. Lines designed with longer heads are best. Some will measure more than 65 feet from the front to the end of back taper. Manufacturers sometimes indicate such lines are for distance casting. After false casting and releasing the line toward the target, the thick portion of the head exiting the rod tip easily supports the bottom of the loop and a smooth long cast results. Double taper lines have a short taper at the front and back, but the rest of the line is relatively large in diameter. If you are interested in just long-distance casting using full fly lines, these do the best job. They do have drawbacks for many fishing situations, and so most fly fishermen prefer the longer tapered lines for a combination of distance and fishing.

Tournament casters early in the 1900s determined that shooting tapers were the easy path to distance casting. More commonly called shooting heads, they are relatively short, heavy sections of line (floating, intermediate, or fast sinking line) attached to a super-thin line. By false casting only the head and releasing it, the heavy head will carry the thin shooting line a greater distance. During false casting, a small amount of the thin running line is outside the rod tip. The distance from the rear of the shooting head to the rod tip is called overhang. If too much of the thin shooting line is outside the rod tip, then it can't support the unrolling loop.

Some floating lines have a short heavy head section and the rear of the line is thin. This allows the angler to false cast the relatively heavy, short head (such as in bass bugging or saltwater fishing) and then shoot to the target. The short,

heavy section easily pulls the thinner running line to the target, obtaining the desired distance on the cast. Such lines when measured from the front end to the end of the back taper will rarely exceed 45 feet, and the remainder of the line is thin. Lines of this design are not the best for casting distance because the extra-thin line at the rod tip cannot support the loop of heavier line, and it will tend to collapse and create shock waves in the line, reducing possible distance.

The Stop

Remember that the casting stroke is comprised of a relatively long and continuous acceleration followed by a quick speed-up-and-stop. The acceleration causes the line to travel much faster, and the faster the acceleration, the greater the line speed. If the rod stroke is short, only the upper portion of the rod bends, but the longer the acceleration, the greater the line speed and the more the rod bends, so additional energy is stored for the final moment of the cast. Once the rod straightens on the speed-up-and-stop, the line will go in that direction. This stop is critical to distance casting, which is why stronger people can cast distances over 100 feet. They have the muscles to rapidly accelerate and stop a rod.

The more false casting you do, the more likely you are to have a disaster. Really good casters make one or two backcasts, and then they let the line go.

If you haven't before, try throwing an apple or potato off a stick. If you just come forward and throw it easily, the potato doesn't go very far. If you come forward, and just at the last minute, accelerate fast and to a hard stop, the potato goes an incredible distance. Come forward and follow through on the stop, which most people do, and you take energy away from the cast. One of the greatest mistakes in distance casting is that people, as soon as they stop the rod, continue dropping the rod toward the water, which takes energy out of the cast. A good way to prove to yourself that this is not a good idea is to select a certain amount of line and throw two identical casts. As soon as you stop on the first cast, lower the rod tip and you open the loop and drag line toward the water. On the second cast, stop the rod and count out loud, "one, two, three." The loop will travel to the target much faster and tighter.

Tight Loops

Loop size is critical for distance. The most efficient cast unrolls the line directly away from the target and then back toward it. Large loops steal distance and efficiency in three ways. A large loop directs the cast's energy around a curve instead of at the target. Large loops need to be held up, and the energy to support that upright loop could have been better used to help the loop get toward the target. Large loops also have to penetrate more air. On a calm day most anglers think this isn't a problem—but air that blows toward you is wind.

The rod tip must stop while it is rising to make a flat backcast with a tight loop.

Loop size is determined at the end of the cast. Back and forward casts are the same; they just go in different directions. I will discuss the forward cast because many think it is easier to visualize. Once the rod bends as it sweeps forward, the line is aimed directly at the tip—with no sag. The rod hand may be moving forward in a straight line or plane, but it really is the base or pivot as the rod sweeps forward. The rod tip is not moving straight ahead but traveling in a slight arc. After the line has been accelerated forward, if the speed-up-and-stop is very brief (remember that the tip is traveling in a minor curve or arc), then it drops slightly below the oncoming line. With a longer speed-up-and-stop, the rod drops lower than the oncoming line and a larger loop results. The more wrist movement in the speed-up-and-stop, the more likely you'll create a larger loop.

Aerializing Line

The amount of line you false cast plays a role in how far you cast. If you want to cast 90 feet and false cast 40 feet of line, the energy of the cast has to drag 50 feet through the guides to the target—not likely. But if you false cast 60 feet of line, the rod loads deeply because of the increased weight and you only need to shoot 25 feet of line.

To pick up a lot of line, the key is to not make the backcast until the line end leaves the water. If any line remains, you have to use energy to pull the line free from surface tension. Many try to take the rod back at a near-vertical angle. At this angle you can't bring the rod far back behind you, so you don't have a wide range of motion to lift a lot of line from the surface. Because of this limited stroke, many anglers simply begin the backcast while the line is still on the water, or during the speed-up-and-stop, the rod tip travels down and back, cre-

ating a large loop and often deep sag in the line, affecting the efficiency of the forward cast.

To make a desirable, fast, flat backcast when picking up a long line, the rod tip must speed-up-and-stop while it is rising—and all line should be free of the water (not the leader—just the line). If you are facing the target, when the rod gets at a right angle to the target, the tip of the rod needs to be below your head.

There are two advantages to this movement. By moving the rod sideways, you can take it much farther back than in a vertical position. This permits you to remove all the fly line from the surface. Also, if the rod tip is lower than your head when it passes beyond your body, it can still stop while rising, creating a flat, fast backcast. With this motion and a good double haul, you'll be able to get more distance.

Shooting Line

It's hard to pick up and cast the entire fly line, so you need to shoot line on your forward cast for a long-distance cast. To shoot a lot of line on a long cast, you need to carry more line in the air to deepen the bend in the rod. Even if you are a really good caster, if you have 35 feet of line outside your rod tip and you are trying to shoot to 90, two things are against you: You don't have enough weight to really bend that rod, even though you are accelerating very rapidly forward, and you are going to have to shoot almost 55 feet of line. If you want to make a longer cast, carry more line outside the rod so that you can bend the rod more deeply and have to shoot less line.

Many skilled casters also shoot line on their backcasts. When you are retrieving line to make a cast, you need to have a certain amount of line out of your guides before you can shoot any amount of line, and the more line you have out, the

CLEANING FLY LINES

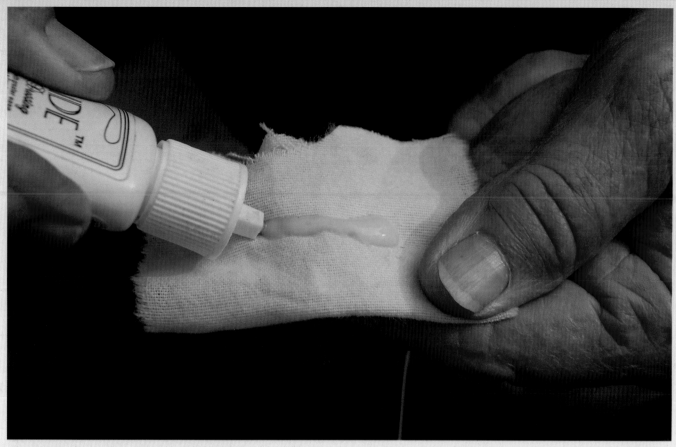

After cleaning your line, dress it with a lubricant such as Glide for the best results. Don't be frugal and use a product not designed for fly lines.

Regardless of the line you use, one of the important factors in good line performance and casting farther is a clean line. Dirt and grit coating the line create undesirable friction as the line flows through the guides and sink the tip of the floating fly line.

To help anglers shoot more line, manufacturers add a lubricant to the lines so they will flow better through the guides. They do this in two ways. Some add a lubricant that is distributed throughout the line, and if some is removed from the surface, the lubricant has the ability to redistribute itself throughout the line. Other manufacturers coat the line with a lubricant. It is important to know which process is used when cleaning lines. For the lines with internal lubricants, line manufacturers sell a scouring pad that can clean the line even if the line is wet. You fold the pad around the line, and draw the line through the pad (squeezing it against the line slightly) to remove the dirt. But such pads should not be used with line that is coated with lubricant, since the pad can scour away part of the lubricant. Contact the manufacturer of your line to find out what they recommend for cleaning.

Manufacturers also offer different materials you can apply to fly lines to make them slicker and shoot better. I recommend sticking with products designed for fly lines. Anglers have tried all sorts of home remedies, including Armor All, which is a vinyl cleaner used mainly to clean and refurbish vinyl in automobiles. It is a cleaner, so it will remove the lubricant on the outside of a fly line. If you apply it too often, it can reduce the effective amount of lubricant on or in the line. Armor All is also water-soluble. When first applied, the line is super-slick and shoots well. The slickness disappears soon after fishing simply because water washed it off the line.

There is one safe cleaning method for all fly lines. Fill a container with warm water and add a few drops of soap. Detergent may remove some of the line's lubricant, so make sure it says "soap" on the label. Immerse the fly line in the warm, soapy water and then scour it clean with a piece of terry cloth or old towel. Once the line has been cleaned, place it in clear water, and with a new piece of cloth, scrub it thoroughly to remove all soap. Any soap residue left will cause a floating line to sink.

You can shoot line on both your back and forward casts. It is good practice to shoot line through your fingers for accuracy and to prevent tangles, but for longer distances you can let go of the line (and hope it doesn't tangle on you!).

more you can shoot. If you have 20 feet of line inside the guide and you are trying to shoot to 40 feet, you can't load the rod. As you make a normal backcast, haul fast and let the line flow through your thumb and fingertips, shooting line. Trap the line and begin the forward cast just as the line starts to slow down when it shoots through your hand. If necessary, sometimes you need to shoot line again on another backcast to get a lot of line out. Hauling is critical for this technique because you need enough line speed on the backcast so that you can drag line through the guides to increase the length of the backcast.

One possible fishing situation where you'd need to shoot line on the backcast is if you've stripped the fly line in and the fish follows your fly but turns away from your fly. You only have a short amount of line to pick up, but you want to make a long cast, so you shoot some line on the backcast, make a forward cast, shooting line on the forward cast, shoot even more line on the backcast, and now you have enough line outside your rod tip to generate the mass necessary to carry the line to the fish.

Trajectory

When casting floating lines, you should stop the rod so that it is climbing slightly above your head. With weighted lines, which fall faster than floating lines, make your forward cast at a much higher angle than you naturally would, well above your head, which means a low backcast. If you stop the rod slightly behind you, before your hand reaches your body, you can throw an elevated cast, which will unroll above your rod tip, and you can avoid hitting yourself in the head.

LONG OVERHEAD CAST

This is the most popular method of making a long cast. The rod moves a short distance before the backcast is made, which requires a good bit of power to throw a long backcast. This method makes it difficult to make long casts if you are not strong. This technique also involves flexing the wrist, and by elevating the elbow off the shelf, the rotator cuffs are stressed in both the back and forward casts. I can't flex my wrist as much as I used to be able to do—when I cast in this manner when I was younger, I would bend my wrist during the drift so that the rod was almost parallel to the water.

Long Overhead Cast

Hold the rod low to start the cast.

Raise the rod vertically to begin drawing on the line.

Continue to lift the line. A common mistake when making any backcast with a long line is to begin the backcast before the end of the line leaves the water. If some of the line is on the water when you make the backcast, you have to rip it free of surface tension, which takes energy away from the backcast and may produce shock waves in the line.

The moment you lift the line end from the water, make the backcast. Hauling on the backcast helps develop enough line speed to make a straight backcast without sag.

At the end of the single haul, my line hand is well away from the rod butt. If the hand remains there, two problems can occur. One, on the forward cast the line will frequently tangle in the reel or rod butt. Two, as the rod hand moves forward, it pushes line slack between the rod butt and the distant hand. This slack must be removed before the forward cast can begin.

As soon as you stop your haul hand, it should begin moving toward the rod butt. If you allow the line loop to unroll well away from the rod, your hand can drift to the rear, with the rod aiding the forward cast.

Just before the backcast line unrolls, your line hand should be close to the rod as shown.

Your rod hand is close to and just in front of the rod butt—perfect position for an efficient haul.

The entire time the rod is accelerating forward, your line hand should be hauling on the line.

When your rod hand speeds up and stops, your line hand should stop hauling at the same time. If your rod hand continues to haul—as so many anglers do—the rod tip doesn't stop but directs some of the energy of the cast downward. How fast you stop after accelerating forward greatly influences how far the line will go.

Allow the line to unroll well away from the rod tip before lowering it. If you follow through with the tip immediately after the speed-up-and-stop, you divert energy from the cast.

Begin lowering the rod. Just before the line completely unrolls, the rod tip should be in a fishing position.

LONG SIDEARM CAST

When you want to make a long cast, you need to extend your arm well behind you to lengthen the stroke. The longer the rod travels through the stroke, the more it helps the cast. Proper backcast is also critical. Most fly casters use a vertical cast to pick up a long line, but the short stroke length limits how much line they can lift from the water. As a result, almost all long pickups with a vertical stroke require the rod tip to pass to the rear of the angler before the backcast is made. To make a straight backcast, the rod should stop while it is rising. Once the rod tip passes vertically beyond the angler, it is very difficult not to cause the tip on the speed-up-and-stop to travel down and back, creating a sag in the line. The extra force needed to pick up the long line causes the rod tip to dip even farther on the stop, creating a large sag in the backcast. This is evident even among many good fly casters. No forward cast is possible until that sag is removed.

Long Sidearm Cast

Start with the rod low to the water. To make the longest backcast stroke possible, lean forward, reaching out with your rod hand. Make sure to remove all slack from the line. This cast allows more use of the body and develops longer strokes back and forward that generate additional line speed during the extended acceleration and load the rod deeper, storing more energy for the final moment of the cast.

Continue bringing back the rod, keeping your arm on the shelf. The rod continues to load. Wait for the line to leave the water before beginning the backcast.

Begin a low backcast. Raise the rod rapidly to lift line from the surface and wait until all the line is out of the water before making the backcast. If some line remains on the water as the cast starts, the rod bends, pulling on the line held by surface tension. Then as the line leaps from the water, it causes a jolt to the rod, creating shock waves in the backcast.

Note in the photo how far the rod tip traveled back before I lifted the line from the water. During the side backcast, the tip should be lower than your head when the rod tip passes beyond your body. This allows the rod tip to stop while rising, creating a flat backcast. If the tip is above your head, there is a good chance the rod tip will stop going down and back and develop a sag that must be removed before you make the forward cast. A fast haul during the time the rod is accelerating aids in a long backcast.

After the speed-up-and-stop, you can extend your arm to the rear and even lift it slightly from the imaginary shelf as the line travels back at an upward angle.

As you extend your arm to the rear, shift your body weight to your rear foot. This body swivel helps lengthen the stroke. The line outside the tip is traveling straight and free of sag.

Just before the line unrolls, begin a forward cast. Haul fast as you accelerate the rod forward.

Keep your elbow on the imaginary shelf as your arm sweeps forward, loading the rod.

To obtain the maximum stroke length, delay the speed-up-and-stop until the rod is well forward and the tip stops in the direction the line is to travel.

The tight loop created by a very short speed-up and abrupt stop indicates all of the energy of the cast has been directed toward the target.

You want a flat line when making a long cast.

Let the line unroll.

Drop your rod tip to the water.

SWITCH CAST

This is an extra-long roll cast developed by Spey casters using two-handed fly rods. But like so many other Spey casts, this one works well with a one-handed fly rod, too. When making this cast, pay attention to the amount of line on the water before you make the forward cast. Spey casters call this the anchor. You only need as much line on the water as is necessary to load the rod. The perfect switch cast is when almost all the line is behind you and just the tip of the line anchors near where you are standing.

Unlike with short roll casts where the line should pause on the surface to load the rod, the extended line weight in the switch cast does not require pausing, and in fact you shouldn't pause, as the D loop may start to droop, developing slack. Because you pick up and drop a long line near you, it is advisable to haul on both the back and the forward casts.

Switch Cast

The longer the roll cast required, the more line should be on the water in front of you. Begin with the rod tip close to the surface.

Lift the rod fairly rapidly while tilting it slightly away from your body. If you lift it too fast, you may create too much disturbance on the surface that could frighten nearby fish. Lift too slowly and a sag occurs in the line that makes it difficult to complete the cast.

Watch the line end. When it leaves the water, make the backcast.

The goal is to deposit the line on the surface of the water no more than 10 feet in front of or behind you. To accomplish this, angle the rod and make a short, side, circular motion with the tip. If the circular rod tip motion is made properly, the line end will fall close to you. Only practice will teach you how to position the line end correctly.

As soon as the line falls to the surface and stops, begin the forward cast. Don't pause too long or the D loop may begin collapsing, and you'll have to remove that slack.

Keep your elbow on the imaginary shelf, and accelerate your rod hand straight ahead.

Note that your elbow and rod hand have been kept low, and the forward motion travels straight ahead. If you briefly speed up and stop in the direction of the target during the final moment of the cast, a tight loop is formed that delivers all the energy to the target.

When the rod tip stops, do not lower immediately, or the loop is opened and energy directed downward, detracting from the cast.

When the line has unrolled well away from the rod tip, begin to lower the tip. Continue to lower the rod as the fly nears the target.

CHAPTER 14

Practice and Teaching Tips

I f you can't shoot well, you can't hunt well. And if you cast poorly, you limit the number of fish you can catch. But the amount you practice doesn't help unless it is good practice. Practicing poor techniques means that you will later have to unlearn your mistakes. Also, don't practice for too long, or you will get tired and your practice will be ineffective. Practice sessions should not be longer than 15 minutes. Two 15-minute sessions are usually much better than an hourlong session. Roll and Spey casts and picking up a lot of line for distance casting can't be practiced in a parking lot, so when possible, try to practice on water. But don't practice while you are fishing; focus only on practicing. You also need to be able to see the fly line, so use a bright-colored one and a cap that doesn't obstruct your view of the entire fly cast, such as some long-brim hats. Also, wear sunglasses to protect your eyes from stray casts.

Practice should also be fun. These are some recommended exercises that help you tighten loops, cast more efficiently, and improve accuracy.

CURING TAILING LOOPS

Tailing loops, when the leader or the front of the line tangles with the main line, plague casters who can cast beyond 45 feet. While tailing loops can occur anytime, they usually develop with longer casts, especially when you make an extra effort to gain a greater distance than you can comfortably cast. You can tail the loop on the back or the forward cast, and some anglers are unaware that they frequently tail the backcast. The resulting knots in the leader are often referred to as wind knots, but they are really bad casting knots. The same angler would get them on a windy day or a calm one.

Remember casting Principle 3—the line goes in the direction the rod tip speeds up and stops. Almost all tailing loops

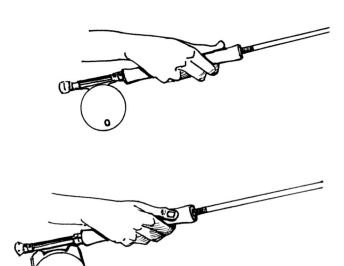

If your rod hand travels at the same height or plane throughout the forward cast and on the speed-up-and-stop the thumb is parallel to the water (vertical or side casting), no tailing loop occurs.

occur when the rod tip speeds up and stops in a straight path, and the line collides into itself. Straight path does not necessarily mean parallel to the water. It can be at any casting angle—the rod tip can stop going up, parallel to the water, or down toward the surface. The most common cause of a tailing loop is elevating the elbow on the backcast and lowering it on the forward cast.

You can also get a tailing loop if the backcast drops so low that it travels below the rod tip throughout the forward cast. Fortunately, almost no one makes such a bad backcast.

For practical purposes, we can eliminate this reason. Some anglers will accelerate forward with the rod, pause, and then begin accelerating again, causing a tailing loop. Fortunately both of these mistakes rarely occur.

Just about everything I have heard and read related to the cause of a tailing loop is misleading. Some common explanations for tailing loops range from shocking the rod during the forward cast, to beginning the forward cast too soon or too late, to moving the rod tip in a concave manner. If you shock the rod with the tip stopping straight ahead, you will get a tailing loop. Shock the rod with the tip descending on the stop, and there will be no tailing loop, no matter how hard you shock the rod. Beginning the forward cast too soon or overpowering the cast and starting the speed-up-and-stop too

late in the cast—all have a tendency to cause the rod tip to speed up and stop in a straight path. If the rod tip travels in a concave manner, you'll get a tailing loop, but this is because you drove the rod handle straight forward.

When we cast a fly, the line unrolls in what we call a loop. As long as the top of the loop remains on the top, and the bottom on the bottom, there will be no tailing loop. When you make a cast in either direction, the bottom of a loop is at the tip of the rod. To eliminate almost all the tailing loops, the rod tip must get out of the way of the incoming line to avoid running into itself. As you come forward in a vertical or angled plane, dip the rod tip slightly on the stop and you will not get a tailing loop. If the rod comes forward sideways, then you must tilt the tip slightly inward.

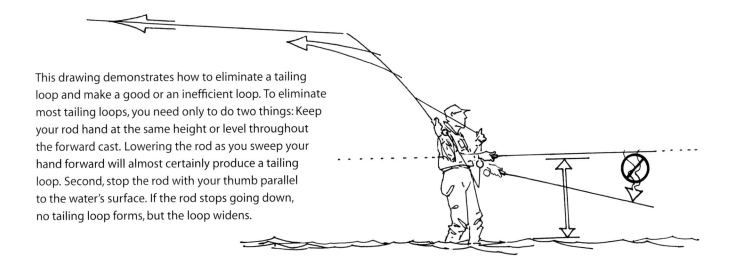

This drawing demonstrates how to eliminate a tailing loop and make a good or an inefficient loop. To eliminate most tailing loops, you need only to do two things: Keep your rod hand at the same height or level throughout the forward cast. Lowering the rod as you sweep your hand forward will almost certainly produce a tailing loop. Second, stop the rod with your thumb parallel to the water's surface. If the rod stops going down, no tailing loop forms, but the loop widens.

Incorrect: Tailing Loop

To teach people how to cast, it is important that you learn to re-create common casting errors like tailing loops. Once you understand and can show people the causes of tailing loops, you can help them fix the problem.

I begin the cast with the rod tip low to the water.

I lift the line for the backcast.

As I make a vertical cast, my elbow rises off the shelf.

I make the backcast with my elbow elevated and the rod hand above my head.

The line unrolls back.

As the backcast nears the end, my rod hand and elbow are elevated.

As I begin the forward cast, I lower my hand and elbow. As soon as the rod bends on the forward cast, the line is aimed directly at the rod tip.

As my rod hand continues to drop, it causes the rod tip to speed up and stop in a straight path. Dropping the rod hand makes it extremely difficult to get the tip to duck under the oncoming line. Because the rod tip sped up and stopped in a straight path, the line behind ran into the line in front of it, creating a tailing loop. The tailing loop will either tangle or create a knot in the line or leader.

Correcting Tailing Loops

From the beginning to the end of the forward cast, your rod hand should travel at the same height toward the target. Beginning with your hand high and dropping it at an angle during the forward cast is the most common reason for a tailing loop. You must stop your thumb parallel to the water, and during the speed-up-and-stop, tilt your thumb down slightly (on a vertical or angled cast) or tilt your thumb slightly inward (on a side cast) to ensure the rod tip will get the bottom of the loop away from the oncoming top line. Your thumb should turn down only very slightly. Obviously, if you turn your thumb down too far, you will open the loop. With either a vertical or side cast, direct your thumb parallel at the end of the speed-up-and-stop to avoid a tailing loop—provided you keep your rod hand level throughout the forward cast.

Avoiding Tailing Loops

Avoiding a tailing loop is simple. Start with the rod tip low to the water. Your elbow should be on the imaginary shelf and your thumb behind the rod handle away from the target. The lower your hand is at the end of any backcast, the more energy can be directed to and from the target. The ideal height for most casts is when your rod hand at the end of the backcast is just above the height of your elbow. The lower your rod hand at the beginning of the forward cast, the less likely a tailing loop will occur.

Lift the rod to draw the line toward you.

Continue to lift the rod while watching the line end.

When the line end leaves the water, make the backcast.

The line unrolls back.

Just before the backcast unrolls, begin the forward cast. Note the height of the rod as the forward cast starts.

Accelerate the rod forward.

Your elbow remains on the shelf and your thumb is behind the rod handle away from the target.

Your rod hand stays at the same height throughout the forward cast. Speed up and stop with your thumb parallel with the surface so the rod tip ducks away from the oncoming line, eliminating the possibility of a tailing loop.

If your thumb points upward on the speed up and stop, the tip will stop in a straight path and a tailing loop occurs (because the rod tip was forced to travel in a straight path). If your thumb points downward on the stop, there will be no tailing loop, but it will enlarge the loop's size.

Casting Block

Tossing a block behind you is often the best way to learn how to make a good side backcast. With most of the casting I teach, I find if you never had a lesson you would do things naturally and instinctively. Imagine you are throwing a block at a target at a slight upward angle directly behind you. With your elbow at your side (not elevated) and your thumb behind the block, simply throw it behind you at an uphill imaginary target. If the block does not go in the direction of the target, you stopped your hand in the wrong direction. To make a good backcast, think about throwing a block in this way, stopping your hand going uphill toward the target. With this prop, I have often been able to teach someone how to make a natural backcast in minutes.

Casting Block

With your elbow in a natural resting position and thumb behind the small wood block, you are going to try and throw it at a target slightly uphill behind you. This will teach you how to make the proper motion for a sidearm backcast.

Release the block toward the target.

For a short cast, sweep your hand back and uphill just a short distance.

For a long backcast, shift your upper body more to the rear, while keeping your elbow on the imaginary shelf. Extend your arm well to the rear before releasing the block at an uphill angle toward the target.

LOOP CONTROL

Once the rod is bent, straining against the line, on either the backcast or forward cast, the line is taut and aimed at the rod tip. While casting, the rod hand is a pivot causing the tip of the rod to travel in an arc. During the speed-up-and-stop, the tip will duck away from the oncoming line. The farther the tip tips away from the line, the larger the loop. The shorter the speed-up-and-stop, the less the rod tip dips and the tighter the loop. You don't cast a fly line—you unroll it away from or back to the target. Many people don't cast tight enough loops, and they also don't understand that it is important to know how to make different size loops to adjust to various fishing situations.

Casting at the Rod Tip

An excellent exercise that quickly teaches people to cast tight loops is having them try to cast at the rod tip. The tip of the rod during a cast travels in a narrow arc, and if you attempt to cast the line at the tip, almost all of the energy of the cast is directed in a tight loop. The line will strike the tip if the rod is stopped too early in the stroke. If the angler ducks or dips the rod tip downward away from the incoming line, a wide loop results.

Strip off about 12 feet of line plus the leader. You must look at the tip during the exercise while false casting and imagine you are throwing the line at the rod tip during the back and forward cast. If you stop looking at the tip and just cast, the exercise fails. Too often when I am teaching, the caster makes a few tight loops and starts to admire them rather than continuing to look at the tip. Inevitably, the loops

In many sports we are taught to follow through, but for tight loops, bring your hand to a dead stop at the end of the forward stroke.

get bigger because the caster is not focusing on the rod tip with the line. It is important that the angler have a background that allows him or her to clearly see the rod tip and line. A vertical cast viewed against a bright sky often makes it difficult. A side or angled cast is usually best.

If I am working with a student, I ask him to relax as I hold his hand and make the first several false casts, emphasizing that the purpose is to make the line strike the rod tip. Once he understands this, I remove my hand. Usually he immediately begins throwing a tight loop. While this exercise is excellent for getting a beginner to throw tight loops immediately, I find that it helps virtually every caster, no matter how experienced, throw tighter loops provided he concentrates on throwing the line at the rod tip.

In almost every sport, we have been taught to follow through, but if you want tight loops, don't follow through after the stop. The bottom of a loop is at the tip of the rod and follow-through simply drags the loop open. This is a common fault with many anglers on their final cast. They will false cast tight loops with no follow-through, and on the last cast as soon as they speed up and stop, they follow through, tearing the loop open. The speed-up-and-stop and the haul should cease at the same moment. Perhaps the most common fault of double haulers is that on the forward cast they continue to haul after the rod stops. Of course, this pulls the tip downward, opening the loop and reducing distance.

Incorrect: Casting Wide Loops

I am beginning the forward cast.

The rod is flexed and the line taut as I begin the speed-up-and-stop.

Because of the long speed-up-and-stop, the rod tip drops well below the taut line.

This causes the line to travel in a wide open loop.

The wide loop creates a sag in the line that I have to remove before moving the line end for the forward cast (Principle 1).

Note how far the rod tip has moved forward and that there is still some sag in the line. I can't begin the forward cast until the rod motion eliminates the sag. When all the sag is out of the line, I can begin my speed-up-and-stop.

A long speed-up-and-stop causes the rod tip to dip quite a ways, causing a large loop.

Casting Tight Loops

As you begin your backcast, the rod is flexed and the line is aimed at the tip.

Make a short speed-up-and-stop to form a tight loop.

Sometimes side backcasts look like tailing loops, but they are not.

Allow the tight loop to unroll.

Just before it unrolls completely, start the forward cast.

Begin the forward cast, loading the rod.

Just before the speed-up-and-stop, aim the taut line at the tip.

The distance the tip drops below the oncoming line determines the size of a loop. Make a brief speed-up-and-stop so the tip only drops a short distance below the oncoming line.

Once the loop unrolls away from the rod tip, begin lowering the rod.

Continue lowering the rod to a fishing position.

Casting Between the Lines

I use this exercise to teach students how to throw tighter loops. It works well for people who have never cast and those who have been casting a long time. In this exercise, the angler teaches himself how to cast tighter loops. The equipment is simple, inexpensive, and easily available. Two 50-foot, $1/4$-inch-thick nylon clothesline ropes work fine, or a pair of 50-foot garden hoses also will do. When I use ropes, I attach long nails to the rope ends, which I then push into the ground to ensure the ropes stay taut during the exercise. In the photos, we are using two fly lines still attached to reels, which also work well.

Stop after every back- and forward cast and evaluate the results of each cast. Don't rush through this exercise.

To teach someone how to cast tighter loops, I set the parallel ropes about 6 feet apart—resembling a pair of railroad tracks. The caster should stand so that the rod tip is about 1 foot inside the nearest rope and ready for a backcast. All casts are made close to the ground. During each cast, he should attempt to keep the fly line and the rod tip inside the ropes. If, at the end of each cast, the rod tip or any portion of the fly line is outside the two ropes, the loop is too large. Every time a backcast or forward cast ends, the caster should stop and examine the effort. When he is able to make a series of casts with the line and rod inside the two ropes, narrow the gap between the two ropes to 4 feet.

When he is successful at this, I have him false cast using sidestrokes, trying to keep the line in the air between the two ropes. Gradually I have him elevate to a vertical position and learn how to throw tight loops from side, angled, and vertical positions. For most students, in 20 minutes they are throwing great loops, and best of all, they are teaching themselves. The caster masters tight loops when he can cast the fly line between two ropes that are only about 30 inches apart.

Casting Between the Lines

Stand far enough back so that the rod tip is just inside the near line at the start of the backcast. Your elbow should be on the imaginary shelf and your thumb behind your rod hand from the center of the parallel lines in front. All casts are made low to the grass, not elevated.

Keep the rod and line low to the grass during each cast.

After the backcast, stop and examine the line. If the line and rod tip are inside the parallel lines, a tight loop has formed. Stop after each cast to monitor what you are doing right and wrong.

Begin the forward cast by keeping the rod and line low to the grass.

This is the kind of cast you are trying to learn—a tight loop delivering the line straight ahead.

This line travels in the center of the two parallel lines because a proper tight loop was made.

This is the result you are working for. By stopping after each cast to examine the line, you are able to make adjustments and soon throw tight loops.

Two mistakes are being made in this practice session. The cast was not directed close to the grass, and it is obvious that this is going to be a large, poor loop.

This is not what you want to do. Both the rod tip and the line are outside the parallel lines because a large loop was created.

If your thumb stays behind the rod handle throughout the cast, all energy is directed straight back and forth as shown.

If you twist your wrist during any cast, it tends to open loops, and energy is directed away from or back to the target.

You'll soon see that twisting your wrist during a cast detracts from its effectiveness.

Twisting your wrist during casting results in a large, inefficient loop and ends with the line and fly well outside the parallel lines.

Once you have learned to make tight loops and keep the rod tip and line inside the parallel ropes, you are ready for the next step. Instead of stopping after each cast, begin false casting above the parallel lines, concentrating on keep the rod tip and line inside on the backcast.

Keep them inside the parallel lines on the forward cast. After mastering the side cast, change to false casting an angled cast and then a vertical cast, and you will soon have mastered the tight loop.

Hula Hoop

In casting clinics I have for years used a hula hoop to help anglers tighten their loops. Even if they can cast tight loops, many can't do so accurately, and the hula hoop is an excellent tool to improve that. Hula hoops come in many sizes, but the standard 32-inch hoop available in many department stores is best to start with.

You can secure a hula hoop to a pole with tape, but often the leader or line snags or tangles between the pole and hoop. I like to have an "arm" extending from the support pole past the top of the hula hoop. The bottom of the hoop should be positioned about 3 feet above the ground.

Without a fly or tuft of yarn on your leader, begin about 30 feet from the hoop and attempt to cast the line (not just the leader) through the hoop. When you are able to get eight out of ten casts through the hoop, back away to 40 feet and repeat. When you can throw at least five out of ten casts through the hoop at 50 feet, you have really mastered loop control. Fly-fishing clubs and groups can have fun by holding informal contests to see how successful members are at throwing a number of casts through the hoop.

When you can consistently cast loops through the hoop at a range of distance from 30 to 60 feet, try casting with your other hand or try casting through the hoop on your backcast.

Hula Hoop

Stand about 25 feet from the hoop for the first practice session. Use a brightly colored hoop and a bright fly line.

As the loop nears the target, you can lower the rod.

Note that the rod tip remains where the speed-up-and-stop occurs. This ensures a tight loop. Fly fishermen quickly learn, when trying to throw through the hoop, that an immediate rod follow-through after the speed-up-and-stop creates a loop too large to enter the loop.

MOUSETRAP

If you want to learn how to throw your fly with pinpoint accuracy, the mousetrap (or rat trap) is the tool for you. Not only is it effective, but it is a lot of fun. I like to print fish names on the trap treadle, such as tarpon, brown trout, etc. Cock the trap and set it about 20 feet from the caster so that it is easily visible. Use a weighted fly with the bend and point cut off. Ideal flies are weighted Woolly Buggers, small Clouser Minnows, or bonefish flies. Use a leader about 8 or 9 feet in length.

Locate the mousetrap about 20 feet away and use a leader of about 9 or 10 feet with a weighted fly. Remove the bend and point of the fly with wire cutters. Set the trap to spring if the weighted fly strikes it. Concentrate on the mousetrap and try getting the fly to strike it. If the weighted fly strikes the treadle, the trap snaps shut and leaps into the air. Even the very best casters fail to hit the trap more than once or twice in 20 casts, but good casters will get close to the trap nearly every cast. Dragging the fly over the trap to spring it doesn't count—you have to hit it with the cast.

Your first few casts may seem to be all over the place, but as you begin to concentrate on the tiny trap, your accuracy greatly improves. One lesson is that accuracy is partially dependent upon concentrating on a small target. Two, you'll become aware that when casting a weighted fly, the leader and fly may tend to curve to the left (if you are right-handed caster). Most right-handers tilt their rod slightly outward on the forward cast. On the speed-up-and-stop, the tip travels in a slight left hook, causing the leader and weighted fly to land on the water curving to the left. To get the leader and fly to travel straight toward the mousetrap (or target), the rod tip must travel vertically during the speed-up-and-stop in a straight path directed at the target.

Mousetrap

The first few casts may be way off target, but as you continue casting the flies, your accuracy should improve. This is because you are now concentrating on the small target. One of the tricks of accurate casting is to concentrate on the exact target area. A good example many hunters understand is if you shoot *at* the deer, you probably will miss it. Hunters have learned to pick a target area on the deer to get a good shot, and it's the same with casting. Don't be discouraged if you miss the trap many times. Even the best casters will probably not hit the mousetrap more than once in fifteen or twenty tries. But most casts will be close.

I have used the mousetrap for years in casting clinics. It is amazing how many really good trout fishermen have played with the mousetrap and suddenly realize they have been throwing an inaccurate curve cast with their weighted nymphs and streamers. Regardless of the angle of the backcast, if the rod is brought forward in a vertical plane and directed at the mousetrap, the line and fly will travel straight toward the trap. But if the rod is tilted as shown here, the weight fly causes the cast to be curved.

The fly will go in the direction the rod tip speeds up and stops. If a right-hander tilts the rod outward on the speed-up-and-stop, the tip flexes inward or to the left. Every cast with a weighted fly will result in a curve to the left.

REFINING YOUR HAUL

In addition to casting on the grass (see page 121), you can also do a few other exercises to improve the speed and timing of your haul. Even if you think you are double hauling efficiently, try these exercises to evaluate your haul.

Two Fingers to Haul Faster

When a fly fisherman needs to make a cast outside his range, the routine usually goes like this: while double hauling, he makes two nice false casts, and then on the final forward cast—as if to give the cast a boost with some extra strength—he powers forward on the cast, often shocking the rod or opening the loop so much that the cast falls far shorter than if he just released the line with no extra effort. Instead of trying to add extra force or power to the rod hand, work on your line hand technique to accomplish this.

Most fly fishermen haul at about the same speed all the time. Instead think of the haul like a gearshift. You should increase the speed of your haul when you need extra distance or speed, such as when casting into the wind, throwing heavier flies, or making longer casts. This makes the line travel faster and deepens the bend in the rod. But if you apply extra force with the rod hand, the forward cast almost always suffers.

When learning to haul extra fast, anglers tend to use extra force with the rod hand, creating shock waves and spoiling the cast. When teaching anglers to haul faster, I ask them to hold the rod with the thumb and first two fingers when false casting. Now it is difficult to use too much power on the cast while hauling extra fast. Soon they realize the extra speed and distance come from the line hand, and they avoid overpowering the rod hand.

Improving Haul: Casting with Two Fingers

Grip the rod with your thumb and two fingers and make your backcast by hauling faster than you would normally. After the backcast, begin with a much faster haul on the forward cast.

Note that three fingers are holding the rod while the line hand is accelerating much faster than normal. Because it is impossible to overpower your rod hand with your thumb and two fingers, the loops are fine—teaching that not overpowering is the key when hauling faster to obtain greater distance.

Speed up and stop.

Note that the line speed is so fast that the line shooting through the guides has actually traveled forward of the butt guide.

Hauling extra fast, additional line could have been shot through the guides.

Improving Haul: Casting with Half a Rod

A rod is a flexible lever, and the longer the rod, the more it helps the cast. Casting with half a rod will quickly show you the limitations of your current hauling technique and force you to improve it. Once you cast better with half a rod, your casting really improves with the whole one. Practice without a fly since the line will often travel close to you.

Improving Haul: Casting with Half a Rod

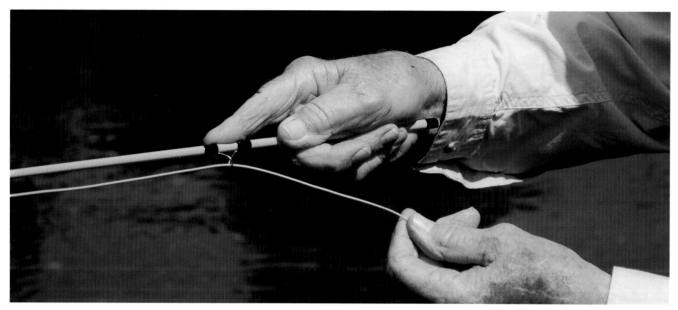

String the line through the forward half of the rod. Because you don't have a handle to hold, you must grip the lower half of the rod tip with your first finger lying along the rod as shown in the photo.

Extend about 20 feet of line outside the rod tip and begin false casting. At first it may not go well because you are trying to cast with your rod hand. Back off on using force with your rod hand and increase the hauling speed, and suddenly the line and rod come alive. With practice, you can cast up to 70 feet with only a half rod.

BACKCASTS

Too many anglers only concentrate on making good forward casts. But making a good backcast is, in many ways, more important. The first main problem that I see with many backcasts is that anglers don't time it properly. During the backcast, if you wait until you feel the tug of the line, the line will be totally extended, and you'll begin the forward cast too late. If a hunter shoots at a flying duck, he aims at where the duck is going to be, not where the duck is when he pulls the trigger. Similarly, you should begin the forward cast while the line loop resembles a candy cane, before it has straightened completely. If there is a popping sound when the forward cast

Before any efficient forward cast can be made, the backcast must be aligned in the direction of the target.

begins, you started forward too quickly. If you wait until the line opens or tugs, the line is falling, developing slack before you can start moving the line forward.

The other big problem with backcasts is making a cast that sags down. To avoid a sag in the backcast, the tip should speed up and stop while it is rising. Anytime the rod tip travels downward during the speed-up-and-stop there will be a sag in the line. The angle the rod tip stops as it rises determines the backcast direction. No forward cast is possible until rod motion removes the sag and begins moving the line end.

A good backcast is elevated and has high line speed, creating nice tight loops.

Whether you cast overhead (above) or sidearm, you want a high backcast. If casting overhead, make a backcast directed up so that by the time the line falls and you are coming forward, you don't tail the loop. There is no sag in the line on this cast even as the loop is almost done unrolling.

Look at your backcast.

Kneeling in Water

When making a backcast while wading deep, sitting down in a canoe or drift boat, or in a kayak, anglers commonly hit the water behind them on their backcast, which spoils the forward cast. This is usually caused by a sag in the backcast line or the line being directed toward the water. Some anglers partially solve the problem by using longer rods to help elevate the sag in the line and keep the line above the surface. But long rods are more tiring to repeatedly cast and unnecessary with good technique. The key to making a good backcast is to stop the fly rod while it is rising so there is no sag in the cast. To accomplish this, begin with the rod tip close to the water, and make a side cast. A good double haul is essential.

Kneeling in Water: Incorrect Backcast

I begin lifting the line.

The rod continues to rise vertically.

When the line end leaves the water, I make the backcast. The butt has passed a vertical position.

I speed up and stop, but because the rod has passed beyond a vertical position, the tip stops going down instead of rising.

This creates a large unrolling loop and sag in the line.

The line as it unrolls is falling toward the surface as the large loop slows.

The line continues to sag toward the water. The longer the line used in the backcast, the more line will contact the water before a forward cast starts.

The line contacts the water as the forward cast begins. This makes it more difficult to make a good forward cast, especially with a weighted fly.

Kneeling in Water: Correct Backcast

The rod tip should be close to the surface.

Begin lifting the line with a side cast, keeping your elbow on the imaginary shelf. Elevating your elbow during the cast tends to drive the line down on the backcast.

As you continue to lift the line with the rod, pivot your body to aid the cast. Haul to help lift the line and load the rod.

The moment the line leaves the surface, speed up and stop and cease hauling.

It is critical that the rod tip stops while it is rising.

This ensures the line will not be diverted downward and there will be no sag. With a short speed-up-and-stop, the loop is tight and the line devoid of sag.

TEACHING TIPS

Don't Display Knowledge, Share It

A good fly-casting instructor should never display knowledge; he should share it. As soon as you try to impress your students with how good you are, you've lost them. The worst thing you can do is cast more than your students while you are trying to teach.

Learn to Say the Same Thing a Different Way

People might have to hear the same thing phrased differently before they understand. This has nothing to do with intelligence; it's just that a certain expression will suddenly convey your point. Explaining the motions of a good forward cast, for example, I sometimes say it's like throwing paint out of a brush or, if my students are from the country, I tell them it's like throwing an apple off a stick. Sometimes I may say that it is like throwing a dart.

Learn to Make Bad Casts

If you can't make bad casts, you don't know what causes them.

Have a Sense of Humor

Humor, especially when it is directed at the instructor, is always welcome. Also humor helps rid tension from the student. For example, if I have a student with a poor backcast, I will often ask, "Have you ever looked at your backcast?" and when they say, "No" I answer, "Well don't." Usually we both laugh and all of a sudden the student is aware he should be looking at his backcast.

Learn to Cast with Your Other Hand

After I tore my biceps in my left arm by turning a mattress, I was lucky that I had learned to cast right-handed. It has helped my fishing and my ability to teach. To show people the correct motions of a fly cast, I often put my hand on theirs and make the cast together. If you are a right-hander working with a left-hander, you're not going to move that left hand the way that you would if you were left-handed. For your own fishing, it's a tremendous advantage to cast with either hand. A lot of times if you are flats fishing and a fish approaches from the right, and you are right-handed, you have to have the guide move the boat around to make the cast. On a lot of trout streams, there are left-hand and right-hand holes.

The Right Age, the Right Tackle

Almost all children under the age of 10 are too young for good instructions. It is not that they aren't strong enough or smart enough—it's their attention span. I suggest children younger than 10 begin with spinning tackle. Younger, weaker people do better starting with a 5- or 6-weight rod, and for stronger people I prefer using a 6-, 7-, or 8-weight rod. The 5- or 6- weight rod is light enough with a light line for them to practice well, but stronger people need a heavier rod and line to aid in bending the rod and developing line speed. Brightly colored fly lines are better to teach with because students can see them in flight. Different colors of lines are best under various light conditions. Always begin teaching with a floating line. Sinking tips and sinking lines are very difficult to start with.

Watch the Line

When I have a student who has never cast a fly before, I don't talk about loop sizes, high line speed, or casting planes. I don't want to overwhelm the student with too much technical jargon. I have him cast slightly sidearm, so he can watch the rod tip and the line. Teaching vertical casting to a beginner is almost like having him cast in the dark—he can't really see what is going on with the line. I tell most people to just throw the line at the end of the rod tip, and I start out on the grass, so that they can stop both the backcasts and forward casts, and slow down their stroke to really be able to think about what is taking place. As they learn to throw at the rod tip, they can then raise the rod tip up and throw in the air, and then eventually I have them cast in every angle—from sidearm to vertical. The rope exercise is very good to either start with or to have them practice after they have the basic motion down, because it allows students to teach themselves, which I think stays with them longer than if they were just being told to do something by an instructor.

Timing the Forward Cast

If I have a student who comes forward too soon or too late after the backcast, I ask him, "Where do you live?" I then have him say the following expression as soon as the rod hand begins to move on the backcast: "Ohio [substitute any state name here] is a good place to be from." If he is coming forward too soon, tell him he is coming forward when he says, "Ohio is a good place." If he is coming forward too late tell him he is really saying, "Ohio is a good place to be from—from—from." This works exceptionally well to about a 40-foot backcast—after that the student should know when to come forward.

CASTING BAMBOO

During the early 1970s my best friend, Irv Swope, and I shot more than five thousand photos for a book on fly casting. While casting fiberglass rods, which eclipsed bamboo because of their performance, we observed that at the end of the cast when the rod speeds up and stops (straightens), the tip makes two distinct up and down flexes and then a series of minor ones before finally stopping. Those two flexes create shock waves in the line that mirror the rod tip's movement. This illuminates one of the reasons that graphite eventually eclipsed fiberglass. The lighter, stronger tip flexed less, allowing more of the energy of the cast to be directed toward the target.

Most people who continue to use bamboo rods despite the advances in rod materials like them for trout fishing because they generally only have to cast short distances, and the flex of the rod makes it more enjoyable to play fish. If you try to cast farther than 30 feet or so, the function of the bamboo rods tends to defeat the cast. Some bamboo rods are designed for longer distance casting, but most of these are so stiff in the butt section that they don't really make good fishing tools.

At the end of the speed-up-and-stop, the heavy bamboo tip makes two major up-and-down flexes—creating shock waves in the line—and then a series of smaller ones. Bamboo rods for trout lines are rather light and so the shock waves are not as pronounced, but they are there. The extra tip weight of bamboo rods that throw heavier lines can cause larger shock waves. It is possible for craftsmen to design bamboo rods for such lines but at a sacrifice. These rods have to be much heavier to better stabilize the tip on the stop.

To cast tight loops with bamboo, you need to modify the conventional up-and-down stroke to reduce the up-and-down flex of the rod tip during the speed-up-and-stop. To make a smoother cast with tighter loops, focus on moving the bamboo rod tip straight back and forth from the target. Tilt your forearm outward at 45 or more degrees before beginning the cast. Your elbow must stay on the same level or plane during the entire cast. If you elevate your elbow and then lower it, the rod tip stops in a downward direction, producing unwanted waves. It helps if your thumb is behind the rod handle away from the target before the cast starts and you never twist your wrist on the cast.

As you bring your rod hand back level on the backcast, shove or stab the rod butt rearward (straight away from the target), never allowing the rod tip to dip. On the forward cast, maintain the rod at the same height through the cast, and stab the rod butt toward the target, focusing on not dipping the rod tip. Stabbing—the motion that you would make if you stuck something with a stiletto, rather than slashed at it with a knife—prevents bending the rod with the arc of your hand, and instead most of the loop is formed by the rod bending against the pull of the line. Because the rod tip stopped in either direction straight away from or toward the target, the result is a flat, tight loop cast virtually free of shock waves. It is important to keep your hand and elbow low through this motion. I have been filmed making this cast with my arm up too high. The following sequence illustrates the popular casting stroke with bamboo rods.

Bamboo Overhead Cast

I am raising the rod to lift line from the water.

My hand and elbow begin to rise as I prepare to speed up and stop.

I begin the backcast. My elbow is well above the imaginary shelf, and my rod hand is elevated.

The forward cast begins.

As I bring the rod forward, my hand and elbow begin dropping.

My hand and elbow drop farther during the speed-up-and-stop. The rod tip has to travel down and around a curve, producing a rather large loop.

On the stop, the weight of the relatively heavy bamboo tip flexes up and down, creating vertical waves.

This creates a large loop, and the shock waves have stolen energy from the forward cast.

The cast unrolls toward the target. If the shock waves produced by the flexing bamboo tip are large, they can tangle the leader and fly.

The cast ends.

Bamboo Sidearm Cast

Modify the basic casting stroke to remove those troublesome up-and-down shock waves. The greater the tip's angle of descent on the stop, the more the weight of the bamboo tip tends to flex, creating the shock waves. The key to the stroke is to stop the tip as straight toward the target as possible and not downward.

Bamboo Sidearm Cast

So that the rod tip travels straight away and back to the target, you need to keep your elbow along the stationary shelf, your thumb behind the handle away from the target, and turn your forearm outward approximately 45 to 90 degrees.

Keep your rod hand at the same elevation. Slide your elbow back on the shelf as the line is lifted from the surface, preparing for the backcast.

Speed up and stop opposite the target. Think about shoving or stabbing the rod butt directly away from the target while the rod hand stays on the same plane.

This creates a tight loop as the tip stops not downward, but traveling straight away from the target. The loop size was formed by how the tip bent under load before the speed-up-and-stop.

Just before the line unrolls, the forward cast begins.

Your elbow slides forward on the shelf, and your rod hand stays at the same level on the forward cast.

Because the tip speeds up and stops going straight ahead, an efficient, tight loop minus shock waves is possible. All the energy of the cast has been directed away from and back to the target.

Do not lower the rod immediately but allow the loop to unroll well away from the rod tip.

If you need to cast a larger loop, which is sometimes desirable, lower the tip slightly on the speed-up-and-stop.

All of the energy of the cast has been directed toward the target.

By modifying your casting stroke, you can cast more efficiently with bamboo and cast much farther than with a conventional stroke.

Bamboo Sidearm Cast with Water Load

If you have trouble keeping the hand level as you bring the rod forward sidearm, try making a backcast so that the line falls straight on the water behind you, and then make the forward cast.

Laying the line on the water behind you lets you make a much slower cast, giving you time to study the stroke. Incidentally, if you want to make tighter loops with conventional fiberglass, graphite, or boron rods, this same practice technique is helpful.

Begin the forward cast by drawing the rod forward against the water tension on the line.

Throughout the cast, move your rod hand forward at the same height above the water, loading the rod against water tension.

Your rod hand continues straight ahead.

Speed up and stop with your rod hand directing the cast straight ahead. During the entire forward cast, your hand tracks flat or straight ahead.

A tight loop and all the energy of the cast are directed at the target because the relatively heavy bamboo tip was stopped going straight and ahead and not allowed to stop downward. The cast is free of shock waves traveling up and down.

The tight loop unrolls the line straight ahead. Because of the camera angle, the line may appear to be tailing, but it is not.

The fly is riding just above a tight loop completely free of undulating waves.

The cast ends.

Index